PENGUIN BOOKS

BAD LANGUAGE

Lars Andersson was born in Gothenburg in 1949. With the exception of the academic year 1972–3, which he spent as a graduate student at the University of Massachusetts at Amherst, he has remained faithful to the University of Gothenburg, where he received his BA in 1970 and his doctoral degree in 1975. He has co-written two books on the local dialect of Gothenburg and is also co-author, with two others, of *Logic in Linguistics*. He has published a book on language typology and several articles on language in scholarly as well as popular journals. Lars Andersson is a lecturer in linguistics at the University of Gothenburg. He is married and has three children and a dog.

Peter Trudgill was born in Norwich in 1943 and attended the City of Norwich School. After studying Modern Languages at King's College, Cambridge, he obtained his Ph.D. from the University of Edinburgh in 1971. He taught in the Department of Linguistic Science at the University of Reading from 1970 to 1986 and is currently Professor of Sociolinguistics at the University of Essex. He has carried out linguistic field-work in Britain, Greece and Norway and has lectured in most European countries, Canada, the United States, Australia, New Zealand, India, Thailand, Hong Kong, Malawi and Japan. Peter Trudgill is the author of *Sociolinguistics: An Introduction to Language and Society* (Penguin 1974); *Accent, Dialect and the School*; *English Accents and Dialects*; *International English*; *Applied Sociolinguistics*; *Dialects in Contact*; *On Dialect*; *Language in the British Isles* and *Dialectology* and other books and articles on sociolinguistics and dialectology.

BAD LANGUAGE

LARS ANDERSSON AND PETER TRUDGILL

PENGUIN BOOKS

PENGUIN BOOKS

Published by the Penguin Group
Penguin Books Ltd, 27 Wrights Lane, London W8 5TZ, England
Penguin Books USA Inc., 375 Hudson Street, New York, New York 10014, USA
Penguin Books Australia Ltd, Ringwood, Victoria, Australia
Penguin Books Canada Ltd, 10 Alcorn Avenue, Toronto, Ontario, Canada M4V 3B2
Penguin Books (NZ) Ltd, 182–190 Wairau Road, Auckland 10, New Zealand

Penguin Books Ltd, Registered Offices: Harmondsworth, Middlesex, England

First published, by arrangement with Penguin Books, by Basil Blackwell 1990
Published in Penguin Books 1992
3 5 7 9 10 8 6 4 2

Printed in England by Clays Ltd, St Ives plc

Contents

ACKNOWLEDGEMENTS

A couple of years ago we decided to write a book together. Since then we have enjoyed many moments of cooperation, and relatively few disagreements. We nevertheless need to thank Jean Hannah for her invaluable assistance in reconciling our two sets of ideas and our two dialects (British English and Swedish English) into one text.

Parts of this book are based on L. G. Andersson's *Fult Språk* (Carlssons Bokförlag, Stockholm, 1985).

The authors and publishers wish to thank the following for permission to use copyright material: The Guardian News Service Ltd for extract from 'Accent leads to receptionist's dismissal', the *Guardian*; A. M. Heath & Company Ltd on behalf of the author, for an extract from *The Changing Room* by David Storey, Jonathan Cape Ltd; The Society of Authors on behalf of the Bernard Shaw Estate for extracts from *Pygmalion* by George Bernard Shaw.

INTRODUCTION:
WHO GIVES A DAMN?

THIS IS A book about language. Who gives a damn about language? Well, you should and everybody should.

Everyone knows that what is being said is important. Answering a question by *yes* instead of *no* makes a big difference – a *yes* should be a *yes* and a *no* should be a *no*. But, over and above this, there are other things. *What* you say is important, but so is *how* you say it.

Listen to what the Bible has to say about it.

> And the Gileadites took the passages of Jordan before the Ephraimites: and it was so, that when those Ephraimites which were escaped said, Let me go over; that the men of Gilead said unto him, Art thou an Ephraimite? If he said, Nay; Then said they unto him, Say now Shibboleth: and he said Sibboleth: for he could not frame to pronounce it right. Then they took him, and slew him at the passages of Jordan: and there fell at that time of the Ephraimites forty and two thousand.
>
> Judges 12:5–6

This shows that language is important. It can even be a question of life and death.

The story from the Bible is an old one, but history repeats itself. There are many *shibboleths* in the language of today. All the sounds, words and constructions discussed in this book are potential shibboleths, i.e. features of language which can be used to identify the speaker as being a certain type of human being – good or bad, educated or uneducated, caring or arrogant, old or young, clever or stupid, English or American, black or white. These identifications do not have to be questions of keeping track of friends and enemies, but they can be.

Introduction: Who Gives a Damn?

What we intend to write about in this book are all those things (sounds, words and phrases) that may be dangerous to use. Language contains explosive items which should be handled with care. The right choice of words may give you the job you want; the wrong choice may keep you out of work.

The purpose of our book is at least twofold. On the one hand, we want to point to where some of the dangers of language use are to be found, where the shibboleths are. We hope that this will keep some readers out of trouble. On the other hand, we want to make a plea for a better understanding of certain linguistic realities. It is our hope that, after reading this book, at least some people will not be as harsh in their linguistic judgements as they have been.

There is enormous variation on every level of language. If modern research in linguistics (particularly sociolinguistics) has shown anything, it is this. And, where there is variation, there is evaluation. We evaluate the variants offered by our language as right or wrong, high or low, good or bad, nice or ugly, and so on.

The more conscious we are about certain types of variation, the more value judgements we connect with them. We have to be aware of the fact that other people may notice all kinds of peculiarities in our own use of language.

WE GIVE A DAMN

We think that questions of language attitudes and evaluation of different language varieties are important. We are glad to have this opportunity to express our views on the subject. At the same time it should be clear that the contents of this book are not merely based on thinking and believing. We build our conclusions and the language ideology expressed in the book on empirical grounds, research, and argumentation.

On the other hand, it is not always enough simply to present the facts. At times we think it is our obligation to state our own

---

Accent leads to receptionist's dismissal

By our Correspondent

Miss Sylvia Turnbull, aged 21, who recently moved to Folkestone from Scotland with her parents, has been dismissed after a month in her new job as an estate agent's receptionist – because according to her employer, people could not understand her accent. Yesterday she described her dismissal as 'silly prejudice' and added that her employer's son-in-law, who worked in the same office, was also Scottish.

Miss Turnbull's mother said Sylvia had a 'pure Scots accent' which was 'a joy to listen to', and that everyone knew what she was saying. The dismissal was a 'slap in the face'.

Mr Evelyn, principal of the estate agency, in Guildhall Street, Folkestone, said: 'It is true that I dismissed Miss Turnbull because of her accent. She speaks very broadly and I, my staff and clients couldn't understand her. My son-in-law's accent has softened with the years'

From the *Guardian*

---

personal view on different matters. When we do, it will be signalled by some kind of 'we think' phrase.

The following lines are taken from Philip Howard's book *The State of Language*.

> I am not an academic linguistician: it is tiresome that we have not yet invented a satisfactory name for the professional students of linguistics. In any case the academics of English faculties have mostly retreated into their private fortress of structuralism. From outside we hear confused and incomprehensible shouts. It is a tragic paradox that, of all academic disciplines, English should have become so impenetrable to those outside the fortress.

Introduction: Who Gives a Damn?

We call ourselves linguists. Since we do our teaching and research at universities, we should probably be classified as academic linguists. However, we do not want to remain secluded inside our private fortress of linguistic theory. We have heard a number of confused and incomprehensible shouts from the outside. But more often we hear very good questions being asked. Here are some examples:

Are people's vocabularies smaller today than before?
Is English changing faster today than it did before?
Is English getting better or worse?

These questions are not normally considered in university linguistic programmes. The reason is, of course, that the questions are either too hard or too trivial, or both. There are no known research procedures which would give us answers to them, at least not conclusive answers.

PARENTS SHOULD GIVE A DAMN

It is easy enough for parents to criticize the language of their children, their loved ones. It is harder to do something about it. Prohibitions and restrictions will not usually help. And there are reasons why it is hard for them to correct the language of their children.

Let us take swearing as an example. In a Swedish questionnaire study, it was found that 75 per cent of the grown-ups disliked swearing and wanted their children to avoid it. However, 75 per cent of them swore themselves. This being the case, it is not hard to understand why it may be difficult to get the message of non-swearing through.

A question of fundamental interest is how parents (and, of course, other people as well) can have such strange views. Why should they dislike things in language which even they use themselves? We think that one very important reason for this is people's constant association of linguistic features with different groups in society.

Parents may have a picture of the world where there are good children and bad children. The good ones are polite, clever and speak nicely. The bad ones are the other way around, and they swear. Of course, you want your own children to be in the group of good children, and on this point we are in perfect agreement. But this picture of life is obviously much too simple.

The important thing for all of us, parents and human beings, to understand is how these attitudes towards language work. Every single person, we think, can list a few things which they dislike in other people's use of language. It may be certain words or certain pronunciations, or even specific grammatical constructions. We all have our favourite elements to hate in language. But, think about it for a while! Why do we dislike this or that aspect of language? Very often, we would say, it is not the language we dislike, but rather the people that we associate it with.

We recommend the reader to do the following. List your pet hates in language. When this is done, figure out why you dislike those particular expressions. If we are correct, you will end up with judgements about human beings as often as with judgements about language.

We – and now we express ourselves as human beings rather than as linguists – happen to dislike the old-fashioned and very posh 'Received Pronunciation' accent. But, of course, it is not really the actual sounds we dislike. Rather it is some of the people who (stereotypically) use this accent. We do not love them as much as we love everyone else.

In this book we mention quite a lot of things in language which people often dislike. We shall try to describe and explain them linguistically. By doing this, we hope to show that there is nothing linguistically strange at all about many of them. They are often bad just because people have decided to regard them as bad.

TEACHERS SHOULD GIVE A DAMN

Teachers are often worried about the bad language of their pupils. This is only natural and, of course, it must be the duty of the school to point out that certain types of language use are not very appropriate in some situations of life.

We should say that there are three different educational policies towards the things we call bad language. Let us call them

1 Elimination
2 Stylistic (situational) differentiation
3 Approval

We shall return to the educational consequences at the end of the book. Here we will only point out that it is not easy to figure out what the best policy is, and the policy must not be the same for all types of bad language. In many cases, we think stylistic or situational differentiation is the best choice. We would take this stand in relation to slang, swearing, expressions such as *sort of*, *ain't*, double negation and many other aspects of language use. In other cases, our stand will be one of approval, e.g. for using prepositions at the end of sentences or *hopefully* at the beginning of them.

WHAT IS SO DAMNED GOOD ABOUT BAD LANGUAGE?

Why should people use what others or even they themselves regard as bad language? Why should we write a book about it? Why not just try to get rid of it, once and for all?

If the things called bad language were all bad and nothing but bad, people would stop using them and eventually they would disappear. The persistence of slang, swearing and all the rest calls for some kind of explanation. There must be some positive values connected with all this bad language. Within sociolinguistics this kind of positive value is usually called *covert prestige*.

The language of the BBC has *prestige*; voices with accents like this are associated with power, education and wealth. These things are highly valued and this explains why so many people strive to acquire the official language.

On the other hand, so-called bad language is often associated with toughness and strength. These latter properties are also highly valued among quite a number of people.

If someone wants to show both that he can afford to drive a Mercedes *and* that he is a tough guy, then he should learn how to switch between the language varieties connected with prestige and covert prestige.

All this gives us, we think, good reasons for writing a book about those features of language which people (all, some or a few) regard as bad language.

I

GOOD OR BAD?

THERE ARE QUITE a lot of people around who love to complain about the language used by *other* people. The pages of our newspapers and magazines, as well as the airwaves of radio and television, are full of complaints about *bad language, bad grammar, bad English, sloppy speech, gobbledygook, bad diction, jargon, slang, Americanisms, mistakes, mumbling, Cockney, affectation, slurring, carelessness* and *misuse.* Self-appointed guardians of the purity and virtue of the modern English language write to the *Radio Times,* the BBC and the national newspapers in a series of desperate last-ditch attempts to stem the tide of corruption which they fear will quite soon engulf the nation in a wave of linguistic awfulness.

When people complain in this vigorous way, however, it is not always entirely clear what exactly it is they are referring to. What precisely *is* 'slang'? What exactly do complainers mean by 'bad grammar'? What is sloppy about 'sloppy speech'? In this book we are going to argue that in many, but not all cases, our guardians actually have nothing to worry about. But, before we can do this, we are going to have to try to sort out just what these different forms of 'bad language' consist of, so that we can differentiate between them as precisely as we can. Then we can indulge in a sensible discussion of what exactly, if anything, is bad about them. We do this here by looking at different parts of the English language in turn – words, pronunciation and grammar – and noting what features under these headings upset people.

THE VOICE OF THE SILENT MAJORITY?

Right to censor

Andrew Collins (Letters 18–24 June) complains that the language was 'butchered' in the recent screening of Apocalypse Now *and I recall a similar letter of complaint following the film's previous showing. Could I for one congratulate the BBC for removing offensive language which neither enhances the quality of the film nor diminishes its powerful effect. To consider bad language 'adult' is infantile. If Mr Collins's adrenalin truly does race in anticipation of its transmission then perhaps he should seek his entertainment elsewhere.*

Meanwhile, let adults lead by example and let us have less offensive language on both television and radio.

(Mr) S J Redfern

Stalybridge, Cheshire

Radio Times, 9–15 July 1988

WORDS

SWEARING

One of the most obvious forms of 'bad' language is, of course, *bad language* – in other words, swearing. Many people are shocked, appalled etc., by swearing. They argue against the use of swearwords such as *damn*, *Christ*, *bloody* and *bugger* on the grounds that they are offensive, blasphemous, obscene, insulting, rude or just unnecessary. We shall be looking at swearing in more detail in the next chapter, but of course it is obvious that people sometimes swear precisely because they *want* to be offensive, insulting etc. There is a lot more to it than this, however.

English is no different from other languages in having words and expressions that no one is supposed to say but that everyone does say – or nearly everyone. Where English may differ from certain other languages is in the *type* of words of this kind that it uses. And the sort of swearing that goes on in a particular language may tell you something about the values and beliefs of the speakers of that language. The famous British anthropologist Edmund Leach, for instance, has suggested that taboo words in English fall into three major groups, which may tell us quite a lot about the preoccupations of the Anglo-Saxons.

1 'Dirty' words having to do with sex and excretion, such as *bugger* and *shit*.
2 Words that have to do with the Christian religion such as *Christ* and *Jesus*.
3 Words which are used in 'animal abuse' (calling a person by the name of an animal), such as *bitch* and *cow*.

It is interesting to note that sometimes words may move from one of these categories to another, or that their status may be unclear. *Bloody*, for example, was originally *by our Lady* (i.e. the Virgin Mary), and thus came into category 2, but it is no longer regarded as 'blasphemy' by most people. Similarly the non-blasphemous exclamations *gee!* (originally *Jesus!*) and *cor!* (originally *God!*) are no longer seen as having a religious origin. The word *damn* may also formerly have had some connection with the word *dam* (meaning animal mother) and thus have been a category 3 word, but most people would now link it to *damnation* and place it in category 2.

HIGGINS (*indignantly*) I *swear* (Most emphatically) I *never swear. I detest the habit. What the devil do you mean?*
Bernard Shaw, *Pygmalion*

With regard to *animal abuse* Leach asks the intriguing question: why is it insulting to call somebody a *pig*, but not to call them a *polar bear*? Leach suggests that this has to do with the way in which phenomena that are contradictory or anomalous in some way are often tabooed: virgin mothers, locks of hair (neither self nor non-self), centaurs, and so on. If you are offended if someone calls you a *bitch*, but not if they call you a *kangaroo*, this may have to do with the fact that dogs, although they are clearly not human, are often in our society associated with humans and thought of as having at least some human attributes. They are therefore, as far as animals are concerned, anomalous.

SLANG

Another sort of language that people often object to is slang. The word *slang* itself is used loosely and in a number of different and rather confusing ways, but we take it that it really refers to words or uses of words or expressions which are extremely informal and which are very often fashionable and therefore rather temporary – they may come into the language, be very popular, and then die out again fairly rapidly. All of us use words of this type, but many people, including teachers, feel them to be inappropriate at least in certain situations because of their often extreme formality. Other people probably object to slang expressions simply because they are new – there are lots of people who are not very keen on novelty. And yet other people dislike particular slang items because they happen to be associated with a social group of which they are *not* a member. Of course, as we shall see later on, one of the points of slang may be precisely to identify you as belonging to a particular social group.

Another of the functions of slang is to make your speech vivid, colourful and interesting, and speakers often seem to keep up with current trends in slang for a while during their lifetimes but then grind to a halt when they can no longer be bothered about whether their vocabulary is fashionable. People frequently give away information about their age and/or attitudes when they speak by how up-to-date their slang is. Just think of the different ways that various generations have expressed their admiration for something.

You could say that something was *top-hole* (pre-war), *wizard* (1940s), *fab* (1960s), *ace* (1970s), *brill* (1980s), and so on, without really meaning anything very different. The difference would lie in what using each word would make people think about *you*.

JARGON

Jargon provides a wealth of complaints about the speech or writing of others. People protesting about jargon normally seize on vocabulary used by other people which they feel is unnecessarily difficult, obscure or complicated. What 'jargon' then appears to mean is this: it is technical, in-group language as seen by non-technical out-group members. One person's jargon seems to be another person's technical vocabulary. In medical language, for example, what in normal language is called 'having your appendix out' is known as an *appendectomy*, your collar-bone is known as a *clavicle*, and your knee-cap is a *patella*. Doctors and surgeons would probably consider this to be perfectly sensible medical terminology, while non-medical citizens might well feel it to be unnecessarily obscure medical jargon. Indeed, it has been suggested that, in countries where medical treatment has to be paid for, a fractured clavicle may be more expensive to mend than a broken collar-bone. It is an interesting question how far we can distinguish between gobbledygook and technical terminology.

MISUSE

Complaints about the misuse of words fall into a number of different categories. First, we can notice objections to *innovations* in the use of words. For instance, many people dislike the use of *aggravate* with the meaning 'irritate', and believe that the original meaning, 'to make more serious', is the only correct one. They find it aggravating that people say *aggravating*.

Secondly, we can note the category of *malapropisms*. They usually occur where rather erudite words are used incorrectly, often because of confusion with other, similar words: for instance in 'There's lots of *condescension* on the windows', where what is meant is *condensation*. Sometimes, as we shall see in Chapter 8, it is a little difficult to distinguish between these two categories.

A third category consists of *euphemisms* ('nicer' words) and other related phenomena, particularly in the speech and writing of politicians, the military and other groups who try to project particular public messages and images. *Making someone redundant*, for instance, is supposed to make them less unhappy than *firing* or *sacking* them; and *neutralizing the enemy* must obviously be much less unpleasant and a good deal more ethical than *killing* them.

FILLERS AND SMALL WORDS

We quite often hear complaints from parents, teachers and others about 'sloppy speech'. These people are sure that the younger generation particularly don't know how to speak properly and, if we are not careful, will vandalize the language as well as the local telephone boxes. 'Sloppy speech' actually seems to mean quite a large number of different things. Something it certainly refers to is the frequent use of expressions such as *well*, *y'know*, *sort of*, *kind of*, and *like*. Many people find this irritating and complain about the inarticulateness of people who say things like

It's, y'know, sort of kind of good, like.

Actually, words and phrases of this type are highly useful in speech, because they help us take time to formulate our ideas, and to keep the floor in conversation. They also give signals and hints to listeners of speakers' meanings and intentions. People who say *sort of* a lot are obviously relatively unsure of their point of view, and/or do not want to impose their views too strongly on the listener. Small words like this are used by all speakers of all languages, including all speakers of English. It simply happens that some people have items other than *sort of* at their disposal. For instance, there are people who, rather than the sentence above, might say

It is, as it were, in my view, so to speak, good, if you follow.

This is really no different from the first version, although it is of course longer, which might be useful if you were taking rather a long time to think of what to say next. Perhaps the most important function of these small words, though, is to mark the organization of conversation, rather as punctuation signals the organization of written texts. We discuss this further in chapter 5.

PRONUNCIATION

It is well known to nearly everybody in the English-speaking world that most of us pronounce the language very badly. But, here again, the strongest complaints are usually reserved for the way in which *other* people pronounce, since it is obviously people from other cities, countries, age groups and social classes who *really* make a mess of things and have the most appalling accents, voices, drawls, twangs, whines and burrs. As linguists, we think that this widespread belief, like so many others that have to do with language, is mistaken. In fact, almost all of us pronounce our native language, whatever it is, very well indeed. We nevertheless acknowledge that there are many uninformed people out there who disagree with us. Once again, we can differentiate between a number of different categories of pronunciations that are complained about.

WORD PRONUNCIATION

Some words in English have more than one pronunciation. Some of us, for instance, say 'ecconomics' while others say 'eeconomics'. This doesn't seem to bother anybody. With other words, however, passions are roused, and one pronunciation is condemned as wrong, illogical, ignorant, ugly and careless, while the other is praised as correct. Should we say 'con*troversy*' or '*con*troversy'? Should it be 'Covventry' or 'Cuvventry'? Is it 'offen' or 'offten'? Does it matter? Will it make any difference to anything important if everyone starts saying 'irre*vocc*able' rather than 'ir*revv*ocable'? In the case of words like *controversy*, where there are two very well-established pronunciations in the community, our view is that *it doesn't matter*. Dictionaries should give both pronunciations, and speakers should feel free to use whichever pronunciation they choose. Of course, where only one pronunciation is in widespread use, the dictionaries will show only this pronunciation, and this single pronunciation is the one everybody should use. If you are not sure how to pronounce *misled*, then your dictionary should tell you to say 'miss-led' and not 'myzeld'.

VOICE

There is very often a lot of confusion in the English-speaker's mind about the difference between *voice* and *accent*. The way we look at it, *accent* has to do with the way you pronounce your vowels and consonants, and with your intonation. *Voice*, on the other hand, is a little more complicated than that. Voice, in fact, seems to have two major components. First, there is the aspect of voice quality that you are born with and that you can do nothing about. People like Pavarotti are probably very happy about this part of their voice quality, but, if you are not, that is just too bad. This is the part of your voice quality that makes you sound like *you*, and that other people recognize you by. It is due to the shape and size of your vocal tract and vocal organs. We are perfectly happy to acknowledge that some people simply have more harmoniously shaped vocal organs than others.

There is also another aspect of voice quality, however, and this is what linguists refer to as voice *setting*. This aspect of voice quality is learned, and may vary from one social group to another. It refers to the habitual setting of those parts of the vocal apparatus over which speakers do have control. One of the most obvious aspects of vocal setting is, of course, the *pitch* of your voice.

People's voices, obviously, do vary quite a lot in pitch, depending on how long their vocal cords are, with men, on average, having deeper voices than women. But, within the physiological constraints imposed by your vocal organs, you can nevertheless choose a particular part of your available vocal-pitch range. (This 'choice' is normally subconscious and made on the basis of what everybody else around you does, but it can be altered if you try hard.)

Thus, it seems that American men, on average and other things being equal, tend to use a deeper part of their available pitch range than British men do. It is not that American men actually have deeper voices than British men in any physiological sense, but that they select a deeper part of the range that is available. If you listen to British men imitating American accents, you will notice that the first thing they do as part of this imitation is to lower the pitch of their voice. They have observed, if only subconsciously, that this difference exists. Similarly, within Britain, people from places such as Liverpool and Birmingham, as well as very aristocratic speakers with 'plummy' voices, are known to have particular settings which are associated with their region and/or social class. These settings have to do not only with the pitch of the voice but also with habitual positions of organs such as the larynx, tongue, and so on.

ACCENT

Accent, on the other hand, has nothing to do with individual physiology, and is entirely to do with learned behaviour. It refers, as we have said, to the way particular vowels and consonants of a language are pronounced, and to the intonation or sentence melodies employed. Because accent refers in this way to pronunciation, everybody, without exception, has an accent. Complainers, of course, often talk as if only other people have accents – and usually rather funny ones at that – but, if they pronounce vowels and consonants when they speak, and we have to assume that they do, they must have accents also. An accent, then, is not something to be ashamed of, because *everyone speaks with an accent.*

Within the English-speaking world, there is an enormous amount of variation in the different accents used – far more than in vocabulary or grammar – and where there is variation there is likely to be evaluation. It is true that we use people's accents to find out things about them. If you can tell whether somebody is a Geordie, Australian, Cockney, upper-class, etc, when they speak, then you are able to do this mostly – and most quickly – from the accent. You may assume that somebody you see in the street wearing strange brightly coloured clothes and chewing gum is American, but you do not *know* that for sure until you hear that person *pronounce* something.

But we do more than use accents as clues. We also pass judgements on them. We say that some people are 'nicely spoken', that others are 'affected' in their speech, and that yet others have 'ugly' accents. As linguists, we believe that judgements of this type are almost entirely social judgements, based on what we know, or think we know, about the accent in question and where it comes from. We do not believe that these judgements are in any way truly aesthetic. But we shall wait until chapter 7 to argue this case. As for the claim which we saw outside a church that 'No language is as eloquent as a good life', we have no opinion – we leave that to higher judges.

DICTION

Diction is quite hard to write about because we are not always sure exactly what complainers mean when they use this word. In any case, it would be easier to discuss this topic on a recording than in a book. One of the clues we have, however, is that complainers often single out certain foreigners who are good at English, and compliment them on having better diction than natives. Our best guess is therefore that *diction* has to do with the fact that slow and/or formal speech has a number of characteristics which differentiate it from fast and/or informal speech. None of us, including the most ardent complainers, uses exactly the same sort of pronunciation when we are talking to close friends in, say, the pub as when we are indulging in public speaking or something similar. Informal, relaxed situations where everyone knows everyone else tend to produce casual, relaxed, fast, fluent, normal everyday speech. This sort of speech is typically full of reduced pronunciations and rather complicated articulatory speech processes which only fluent native speakers have learnt how to do properly. Poor old foreigners will probably never master these forms, partly because they can never manage to speak the language fast enough. In English, one of these fast-speech processes is *assimilation*. This means making two adjacent sounds more like each other, as in *bab man* rather than *bad man*, or *goob boy* instead of *good boy*.

We can note also the *reduction* of unstressed vowels to the *uh* vowel (which is the most common vowel sound of all in English), as well as the total disappearance of vowels and consonants in unstressed positions. This is especially common in words such as *not, have, had, can, would*, which are very often unstressed and which can appear as *n't, 've, 'd, c'n*. Anyone who went round saying *I would nott havv done that* or *I cann nott see that* would sound very strange, since these reduction processes are so natural and normal.

And we also find *elision* processes, such as the very common reduction of a series of three consonants to two. Most of us will usually say all the consonants in *West Africa* and *Key West*, but very few of us will actually do so for *West Midlands*. What we will normally say is *Wess Midlands*, without the *t*. This, like other fast speech processes, is entirely normal. Without these processes, speech would sound very stilted and become rather inefficient. However, because these processes are inhibited somewhat in more formal speech on more prestigious social occasions (just as they are when one is speaking on a bad telephone line or to a foreigner who does not understand English well), there is a tendency to think that there is something wrong with them. Actually there isn't, and languages really couldn't manage as satisfactory instruments of human communication without them. Of course, it is absolutely true that schoolchildren can benefit from guidance as to when and how to speak on formal occasions.

GRAMMAR

NEW FORMS

We believe that when complainers use the term 'bad grammar' they may be referring to any one of three rather different types of language. They may, first of all, be suffering from a fear of grammatical *innovations* in the English language. Sentences such as

Hopefully *it won't rain tomorrow*

were not used in Britain (although they were in the United States) before the 1970s, and, although this usage is now extremely common, some British people still object to it. We shall discuss this type of phenomenon further below, although it's hard to say why people get alarmed in this way. We don't know why they do, but we would like to assure them that innovations of this type are a good deal less dangerous than innovations such as atom bombs and laser beams.

LATIN INFLUENCE

Secondly, it is surprising but true that many English speakers are still under the influence of Latin, a language which has not had any native speakers for centuries. We shall look at this in more detail in chapter 6. When people object to grammatical forms which have been perfectly normal in English for several hundred years, such as

It was me that did it

the real reason is that the Latin equivalent of *me* could not be used in this way.

SOCIAL DIALECT

Thirdly, and perhaps most importantly, we also find many objections to grammatical forms which happen to be typical of the speech of speakers from a lower rather than higher social-class background. Again, many of these forms have been around in the language for hundreds of years. Thus, as we shall see in chapter 6,

I don't want none

is not actually 'bad grammar' in any meaningful sense of the word *bad*, but in twentieth-century English it is not found in upper-class or middle-class dialects of the language. Although they usually do not realize it, this is why many people, including especially teachers, argue against such constructions. They have been very imaginative in inventing other reasons to justify their opposition.

PRESCRIPTIVE AND DESCRIPTIVE GRAMMAR

People do not always do what laws, rules and customs tell them to do. We know that we should not cross the street when the light is red. At the same time, we all know that people once in a while do not follow this rule. There is a difference between what we should do and what we do.

It is much the same in language. There are rules or grammars prescribing the forms people ought to use when they speak and/or write (*prescriptive grammars*). And there are rules or grammars describing the forms people actually use (*descriptive grammars*). We believe that prescriptive grammars take subjective statements about attitudes to language and attempt to make them into objective statements about grammar. Descriptive grammars tell us what the actual language use of speakers is like without any remarks about right or wrong, good or bad.

The grammar books used in schools are to a very large extent prescriptive. Their purpose is not to describe the basics of English grammar, but rather to teach people how to use language. They take the basic grammatical patterns of English for granted and concentrate instead on more peripheral things, because that is where variation is found. Things like *It's I/me, ain't*, and double negation are grammatically peripheral compared to facts about basic word order, for example. An English grammar written for English-speaking people need not say that the basic word order is subject–verb–object, or that adjectives are usually placed before nouns (*big house* rather than *house big*). For many foreigners, however, this type of information is very relevant.

It is not unusual for a prescriptive grammar to explicitly go against common language use. Below is an old example taken from Bishop Robert Lowth's *A Short Introduction to English Grammar* (1762):

> The Preposition is often separated from the Relative which it governs, and joined to the verb at the end of the Sentence ... as, 'Horace is an author, whom I am much delighted with' ... This is an Idiom which our language is strongly inclined to; it prevails in common conversation, and suits very well with the familiar style of writing; but the placing of the Preposition before the Relative is more graceful, as well as more perspicuous; and agrees much better with the solemn and elevated style.
>
> Quoted in J. Aitchison, *Language Change – Progress or Decay?*

A clearer example of a recommendation going against common usage would be hard to find.

THE MAP AND THE LANDSCAPE

Descriptive and prescriptive grammars are not completely different from each other. In reality, even a prescriptive grammar must describe something – the real or alleged language use of the educated classes, the good authors, or simply our elders and betters. This is rather self-evident. We can think of the grammar as a map, and language use as the landscape. Even if the goal is to make a prescriptive grammar, the map cannot be completely disconnected from the landscape.

Suppose that we want to make a descriptive grammar. Our goal is to make the map as accurate as possible. But this is not so easy. The linguist faces a problem which the cartographer does not have. A mountain has the same height no matter who measures it. It is possible that John Smith inflects his verbs in the same way no matter who he is talking to, but not even that is certain, as modern sociolinguistics has taught us. However, it is not the task of linguists to describe John Smith's language. We want to describe everyone's English, and so we are forced into a lot of generalizations, some of which may be hard to make, some of which may be rather crude.

Modern linguistics is a descriptive science. Linguists describe how people use language in real life, not how they ought to use it. In practice, it is not always evident that it is really common usage that has been described, but in principle linguistics is descriptive.

AIMS OF THIS BOOK

This book has a descriptive aim. But how can a book about attitudes and bad language be descriptive? There is not really a contradiction in this. People's attitudes to language, as with everything else, can be described without any personal evaluations from the describer.

We shall try here to describe the attitudes of the speech community. However, once in a while, as we said above, we shall state our own opinions, for it would be wrong or cowardly of us to hide ourselves behind theories and descriptions. When we state our own views, we shall say that we do so. It should be clear from the text which are our own views and which are descriptions of other people's attitudes. There are good reasons for taking a serious interest in attitudes to language. They play an important role in the life of language. Let us take just one example.

NORMAL VERSUS ABNORMAL LANGUAGE

Suppose we make a distinction between normal and abnormal use of language. The borderline between the two types is not clear. Normal language use is the speech behaviour of ordinary people – rich or poor, short or tall, male or female, young or old. If something is called an abnormal use of language, this does not mean that it has to be a serious or dangerous condition. It only means that the phenomenon in question does not belong to any conventionalized variety of the English language.

Many things belong to the abnormal use of language. Brain injuries can result in more or less serious aphasia, even a total loss of language. Far less serious, but still abnormal, are lisping and stammering. These things do not belong to any dialect or any other variety of English; therefore, they must be considered as abnormal. This does not mean that we have to call for an ambulance or start gigantic compensatory programmes. For some people, extensive stammering may be a serious handicap, but in slight forms it is nothing to worry about.

The great part of language use that we meet must, of course, be classified as normal language. This normal language use can be subdivided into, on the one hand, the good, correct and accepted; and, on the other hand, the bad, incorrect and unaccepted. It is this latter type of language that we shall discuss in this book.

One good reason for paying special attention to this second type of language use is that many people show a tendency to regard is as abnormal. No matter what we may think about swearing, no matter how much it hurts our feelings, we must regard it as normal.

The reason is, of course, that it forms part of many varieties of English; and not only English – we find it all over the world. And there is nothing mentally wrong with people who use double negatives like *He doesn't understand nothing*. They know the difference between *yes* and *no* like everyone else. They can even be good mathematicians. There will be more about all this later.

But let your communication be, Yea, yea; Nay, nay: for whatsoever is more than these cometh of evil.

Matthew 5:37

Obviously, human communication does not always live up to the good standards of Christ's Sermon on the Mount.

TRULY BAD LANGUAGE

In most of this book, we shall be making the point that language that is often thought of as being 'bad' in some way may not necessarily be bad, or is bad only in certain contexts or in certain respects. This does not mean, however, that there is no kind of language that we believe to be bad. For instance, the American linguist William Labov has placed the two concepts *verbality* and *verbosity* in opposition to each other. Verbality refers to speaker's abilities to dress their thoughts in words, to express themselves. Verbosity refers to speakers' abilities to keep a conversation going without really saying much. We should, of course, in the name of honesty, admit that we all have our share of both verbality and verbosity, but the proportions may differ. The worst thing is that it is sometimes hard for the listener to decide which is which – words with content or words without.

Many a politician has proved that well-polished, nice-sounding language may be devoid of content. An interesting fact is that we often do not detect the emptiness and inconsistencies until we get a speech on paper and analyse it. A politician may, for example, declare with great emphasis and a sincere tone that 'All the necessary steps will be taken'. This sounds good – but what could be more obvious? If it is necessary to do something, it must by definition be done. It is only when we sit down and think about it that we realize that the politician has not actually given any details about what steps would be taken or who will take them.

Truly bad language: this is just an example and more examples are not hard to find – unfortunately.

If the assets consists of stocks or shares which have values quoted on a stock exchange (but see next paragraph), or unit trust units whose values are regularly quoted, the gain or loss (subject to expenses) accruing after 6 April 1965, is the difference between the amount you receive on disposal and the market value on 6 April 1965, except that in the case of a gain where the actual cost of the asset was higher than the value at 6 April 1965, the chargeable gain is the excess of the amount you received on disposal over the original cost or acquisition price; and in the case of loss, where the actual cost of the asset was lower than the value at 6 April 1965, the allowable loss is the excess of the original cost or acquisition price over the amount received on disposal.

If the substitution of the original cost for the value of 6 April 1965, turns a gain into a loss, or a loss into a gain, there is, for the purpose of tax, no chargeable gain or allowable loss.

General Guidance (leaflet on Capital Gains Tax)

Verbosity may also be a usable skill at school. One of us had a classmate who could always give an answer. If the teacher asked,

'What was the political situation in Poland around the middle of the eighteenth century?' most of us who had not done our homework answered, 'I don't know'. But not this pupil. He always managed to construct an answer like 'the political situation in Poland around that time was characterized by internal schisms and external tensions'. Something like that is usually true. We must, of course, admit that the answer points to a pretty good language capacity. But this may not be the ideal or optimal way of using our linguistic abilities.

Language can also be truly bad in other ways. We believe, for example, although we shall not be discussing these issues further in this book, that racist and sexist language are highly undesirable, to say the very least. It is worth pointing out, however, that in these cases language is a symptom, not a disease in itself. Abolishing racist language will not necessarily abolish racist thinking. And encouraging non-sexist language will not in itself lead to sexual equality, although we agree that drawing attention to sexist language – such as the use of the pronoun *he* where both males and females are involved, or defining *doctor* as 'a *man* of great learning' – can be a useful thing to do. Drawing attention to the symptoms can make people more aware of the disease and more inclined to take steps to combat it.

Good or Bad?

> *The word* free *still existed in Newspeak, but it could only be used in such statements as 'This dog is free from lice' or 'This field is free from weeds'. It could not be used in its old sense of 'politically free' or 'intellectually free', since political and intellectual freedom no longer existed even as concepts, and were therefore of necessity nameless. Quite apart from the suppression of definitely heretical words, reduction of vocabulary was regarded as an end in itself, and no word that could be dispensed with was allowed to survive. Newspeak was designed not to extend but to diminish the range of thought, and this purpose was indirectly assisted by cutting the choice of words down to a minimum.*
>
> George Orwell, *Nineteen Eighty-Four*

2

ATTITUDES

BAD LANGUAGE IS a far from clear and unambiguous concept. There is an aesthetic dimension to it which relates to the distinction between the ugly and the beautiful. It also has a moral dimension relating to good and evil. Maybe there is also a hygienic dimension, approximately clean versus dirty. There may be even more distinctions, such as stylish–shabby, right–wrong, high–low.

These distinctions are, according to the anthropologists Mary Douglas and Edmund Leach, related to each other. Furthermore, these researchers claim that such distinctions and concepts are closely tied to the culture we live in. This means that the culture, or the ideology of the culture, decides what is right, noble and good. Nothing is good or bad in itself. No word or phrase is in itself bad. It is bad only in the eyes of those who evaluate and look at the language.

If we turn the argument around, we can say that what is judged as bad or wrong in a certain culture reveals something about this culture. This is one of the better reasons for taking a serious interest in bad language, or, rather, people's ideas about bad language.

Human beings are products of nature and culture. We are undoubtedly born as children of nature. We eat and shit, belch and fart, sleep and scream. Through our upbringing we acquire several cultural patterns which among other things will make us into more social beings. We learn that certain things are eatable while others are not. Just think about how disgusting we regard even the thought of eating dogs, cats or worms. Nevertheless, a good cook could probably make dog taste as good as pig. In other cultures it is considered disgusting to eat pork.

Most things connected with the borderline between our own

body and the outside world evoke feelings of filth, disgust and shame. Everything that leaves the body at different places and in different ways (faeces, urine, mucus, sweat, menstrual blood, spittle, semen, ear wax and all the smells of the body) are things which we are supposed to be afraid and ashamed of. They are to be hidden away and not to be talked about. (Tears are a notable exception.) There is a desire, even an obsession, in our society to keep our bodies clean. We wash ourselves and our clothes many times more than people did a hundred years ago. Showers, washing machines, hot water and more clothes make it so much easier. Hygiene has improved and tuberculosis is no longer a plague in the modern world. There is a horror of contamination. Food is wrapped up in plastic and we want our plates and glasses to be clean, extremely clean.

There is also a desire on the part of some to keep their souls clean. A Christian life is supposed to help us to keep clean inside. According to the Christian religion we cannot do this by ourselves, but we can get absolution. This can perhaps somewhat blasphemously be seen as an internal bath. People who say they are not religious also follow a number of rules of conduct which resemble the Christian ones.

In addition, there is a desire to keep the language clean. Many people want to throw out the filth, the dirt and the blaspheming from their language. Others want to free their native language of the 'contamination' of foreign influences. Many people all over Europe are afraid of the impact of the English language on their respective native languages. The British are often hostile to American influences. The Americans need only be afraid of themselves, linguistically that is. Some people want even more standardization in an already standardized language.

Body, soul and language – we want them all to be clean and nice. Our point is that these things go hand in hand. What all this means is that it is hard to know how people have built up their ideas about bad language and that these ideas may be related to very basic ideas in the culture about purity and cleanness in general.

People are supposed to be clean when they go to church. They also clean up their language when they go there. Both working clothes and slang are left outside the Lord's house. This pattern is even more obvious in Islamic countries. Muslims wash themselves before entering the mosque and they leave their shoes outside. Religions of different types often have sermons or prayers conducted in a language which fundamentally differs from the ordinary spoken language. This language is certainly not considered bad. Rather it is a sacred language. The Arabic of the Koran is but one example. Even in Protestant cultures, where it is essential that the sermon is conducted in the language of the people, the religious language is somewhat archaic. New translations of the Bible are always met with scepticism from a lot of people.

People tell each other to clean up their language rather in the same way as they talk about dressing up when going to a party. You wash your armpits, put on a clean shirt and use deodorant to keep away the sweat and the bad smell. When we dress up and go somewhere to make a good impression, we also leave our dirty language at home, if we have any.

It can be seen from people's reactions that they do not keep the purity of body, soul and language apart. Most people would not be surprised if a sloppily dressed man in his working clothes cursed and swore. You would perhaps be more surprised if he opened his mouth and sounded just like an MP arguing for increased tax reductions for stock-owners. Likewise many eyebrows would be raised if a BBC reporter looked and sounded like a football player entering the locker room after a tough game on a rainy Saturday in November. A lot of people react in about the same way to dirt, untidiness, immorality and bad language, with the same faces, frowns and wrinkling up of the nose.

ONCE UPON A TIME

All over the world there are children acquiring their native language. They look like slow starters, beginning to talk at between twelve and eighteen months. They learn one or two words a week.

Their vocabulary grows, like their grammar, but slowly. Then, around two years of age, there is a veritable explosion in the vocabulary. Parents often cannot understand where they get all the words from. This explosion occurs some time between the ages of eighteen and thirty months, but it varies from child to child, just like other faculties, such as crawling, walking and jumping. We are certain that many parents, even those not interested in language, have noticed this sudden growth in their children's vocabulary.

If everything is as it should be, the child's vocabulary grows steadily during the pre-school age, school, adolescence and even during years later in life. Of course, we forget a couple of words now and then, but presumably the number of new words in our vocabularies outnumbers the losses.

However, there is a popular belief that children's vocabularies can be subjected to catastrophes. Such linguistic folklore claims that there are certain words or phrases which impoverish the language. Slang and swearing are often counted among these 'linguistic cancer cells', which is what people seem to think of when they use phrases like 'impoverished language', and 'linguistic deprivation'.

Assume the following. We have a cute little girl called Mary. She is five years old and has 3,693 words in her vocabulary. This figure may seem high but actually it is not unreasonable. (Counting the number of words a person knows is a rather difficult task, and depends very much on what we mean by 'a word'. We lose count already at the time of the vocabulary explosion mentioned above.)

Suppose now that this little girl, through the help of her big brother, learns the words *bloody, damn, shit,* OK and *sort of.* What happens? One could imagine that her vocabulary now contains 3,698 words. However, according to popular belief, it is not that simple. These five nasty words are believed by many people to impoverish the language and the vocabulary. Like malignant tumours, they destroy what comes in their way.

Personally and linguistically, we find it hard to believe that those words are so dangerous. We actually think that our little girl now has 3,698 words in her vocabulary. The main argument is, of course, that every other member of the speech community also has these words in his or her vocabulary. The difference is that some people use these expressions more than others. Since we all know these words, they should be equally dangerous to all of us. Or do grown-ups and educated people have a particularly good linguistic immune system?

Another popular explanation for why these words are dangerous is perhaps slightly more intellectual. According to this view these dangerous words get stuck in our throats and stop us from swallowing more words. Here vocabulary is seen as some kind of container which is filled through a bottle-neck.

Expressions such as *sort of* get stuck in the neck. Other, 'proper' words, such as *law* and *order*, cannot reach the vocabulary. The 'explanation' put forward for this might be that language-users do not see the need for other words once they have learned such handy general expressions as *that sort of thing, stuff like that, and all that sort of thing*. In fact, however, it seems to be vital for our language, like all other languages, to contain general expressions with wide application and little content, such as *stuff, thing, phenomenon, entity* and *property*. These words stand for a whole lot of ... (what do you place in this frame?). Such words are necessary in every language. Some of them, of course, such as

stuff and *thing*, are considered less good than the others, but semantically their function is more or less the same.

Apart from these words, every language obviously also contains thousands of more specific expressions with little application but much more content; for example, *casserole, cassock, creese, crepon* and *claret*. This latter type of more specific word comes in great numbers. Every human language contains a couple of hundred thousand of them, although no speaker of the language knows all of them.

All languages need words on all levels of generality and abstraction. And of course a word does not have to have a wide application and little content, like *stuff*, to be damned by popular belief. The expression *toe-jam* is very specific in meaning. Yet the expression is not met with much approval or admiration. On all levels of abstraction, there are words which are considered good and others which are considered bad.

The critical reader may frown and say something like 'All right, it may well be that all types of words are needed but it is nevertheless the case that many children have too small a vocabulary and use language with far too little variation'. We will certainly agree that many young people – and old people too – have too small a vocabulary. We have certainly not met anyone who knows too many words. What we cannot understand is how a person's vocabulary can *grow* if we *take away* words considered bad. We believe that vocabulary is enlarged by adding new words, not by forbidding the use of a handful of words already learned.

It is also obvious that it is helpful to be able to vary our use of language in both speech and writing. The question is thus one of how variation can be increased, and language improved, by reducing one's vocabulary through the banning of sylistic levels such as slang and swearing. We find it hard to believe that this can be the case.

And, if Mary now has acquired a couple of nasty words, we still think that she has enlarged her vocabulary rather than reduced it. And remember that this story is repeated time after time, even in the best of families.

LANGUAGE ACQUISITION AND ATTITUDES

All children learn their native language at an early stage of life. At five they are pretty good 'native speakers'. They know hundreds of rules and thousands of words. Their grammar is more or less perfect – no matter what parents or teachers may say. This may sound surprising, but it is nevertheless true.

Children know the basics of the phonological, morphological and syntactic systems of language. These are the central parts of the sound system and the grammar. Other parts of the language take more time to learn, in particular vocabulary and pragmatics –

<u>*A true picture? A teacher's view of her pupils'*</u>
background

There is usually a television set which is on, but that is probably better than dead silence or angry words. The child may not get his share of the family food unless he is there when the food is ready, and at the table he is told to 'shut up and eat', for mealtime is not the family affair it is in middle-class homes. Swearing may be practically the only communication among family members, and 'damn' may be inseparable from the preface 'god' in their minds. 'Go to hell' is interiorized in many families in the United States as 'bloody' and 'bleeding' seem to be for some of the British.

Quoted in Cause for Concern

i.e. how to change one's language from one situation to another. We keep learning vocabulary and situation-specific language all through our lives.

If parents and teachers think that children are slow or bad learners of grammar, this often reflects adult linguistic hang-ups, and all of us have quite a few of them. We focus so much attention on constructions like *He can't see nothing* that we do not realize how much children do know when they say such things. They know that the subject goes first, the negative is placed between the auxiliary and the main verb, the form of the auxiliary is *can* not *cans*, and the main verb is in the infinitive form. This is not bad at all. We shall return below to the construction with double negation. (And, to all those who still think that their children are slow learners of grammar, we recommend a course in Finnish or Japanese.)

Language acquisition is part of *socialization*, i.e. the modification from infancy of an individual's behaviour to conform to the demands of social life. Socialization can be described as a process by which a biological being (the new-born baby) is transformed into a social being (the grown-up member of society). There are a lot of things we must learn: respect for the property of others, how to behave, how to hold a knife and fork at the dinner table, how to boogie-woogie, and everything else.

To become a good member of society, we must learn our native language. If we do not, we shall be condemned to a life at the periphery of society. Not only is language acquisition part of socialization; it is also the means by which much of the socialization is transmitted. It is through language that we explain to our children what is right and wrong, good and bad, clean and dirty, and so on.

Children acquire their native language in contact with other people. They can never do it in isolation. There are always people around to help them. Let us make a simple classification of the groups most relevant for language-learning. Every group is important, but in different ways and at different stages of life.

1 Parents, family, relatives
2 Nursery school, school, work
3 Playmates, friends
4 Mass media (TV, radio, papers, books, film, theatre)

The first three groups represent people who the child and later the adult is in direct contact with. There is a lot of two-way communication between the individual and these groups. We hear what they say, they hear what we say, and they can appreciate or criticize our way of using language.

The fourth group is quite different. Mass media represent one-way communication. We listen to what they say, we read what they write, but they do not hear or see us and they cannot condemn or applaud us as language-users. What mass media can do, and do very successfully, is to provide us with a great number of linguistic models, which we may accept or reject, follow or turn away from.

The first three groups are important because we are in direct contact with them. They can even force us to use language in special ways. Parents can punish their children for swearing. Teachers decide what the language rules of the classrooms are (or should be). Many teachers would no doubt like to have stronger or more effective means of controlling the language of their pupils. But they do give out the marks, which is a very strong instrument for influence. However, this does not work on pupils who do not care about marks, and more violent forms of punishment are forbidden and/or out of fashion. Friends are the people who can use the strongest forms of language control. A group of kids can simply tell another child that he had better talk like them or he will be thrown out of the group.

Mass media can do nothing of the sort. Yet they have a strong effect on language simply because they reach so many people so effectively. Every one of us can influence a few people's language a lot. Mass media may influence millions just a little bit and the total effect may be impressive.

The four groups mentioned above are not ranked in order of importance. They are all important but in different ways and during different periods of life. During the first couple of years, the parents and the family are most important. Around the age of seven or eight, school means a lot. If the teacher's word goes against the parent's word, it is the teacher's word that will win in the minds of our young and loved ones. In school, children learn to read and write (hopefully), and they learn to talk about public affairs; to talk not only about their own family, village or town, but about the whole world. In school they learn to think and talk about human beings, issues, problems and events far away in place and time. Step by step their perspective becomes less egocentric. Of course, this process started long before school, since we talk about these matters in our families as well. It is just that this aspect of intellectual development is so central to the school.

In the early teens, friends (or the 'gang') are very important. We suspect that, when kids dress in exactly the same way as all of their friends, they must talk in the same way too. There is a pressure to conform in behaviour, language, clothing and other things. This pressure is always strong but never as strong as it is in the early teens, at least in our Western culture.

The difference between the working class and the middle class is more pronounced in Britain than in America. This is also reflected in language. When sociolinguistic studies carried out in Britain and America are compared, it can be seen that the gap between the working class and the middle class is wider in the British investigations.

The figures below snow the frequency with which speakers from different social backgrounds, in Norwich and Detroit, have been shown to say things like *he go, she run* rather than *he goes, she runs.*

Use of verbs without -s in Norwich and Detroit
(percentage of speakers by class)

NORWICH		DETROIT	
Upper middle class	0	Upper middle class	1
Lower middle class	2	Lower middle class	10
Upper working class	70	Upper working class	57
Middle working class	87	Lower working class	71
Lower working class	97		

MORE THAN ONE LANGUAGE

Language is learned through the help of different groups of people and these different groups use language in different ways. One rather common situation is to find dialectal and 'decent' language used at home, less dialectal but equally 'decent' language used at school, and, finally, dialectal and more 'indecent' (more swearing and more slang) language used among friends.

At pre-school age most people have already learned to use language in a couple of different ways, depending on who they talk with. There is nothing strange or unique in this. It is a universal of language. All languages use different styles of speaking in different situations. How great and how ritualized these differences are may differ from one language to another.

Not only do we learn to use language in different ways. We also learn to view language in different ways. Through the years we acquire, each and everyone of us, a whole ideology of language. We have ideas and hang-ups about slang, swearing, dialects, spelling mistakes, grammatical differences, scientific terminology, pronunciation, the prosody of BBC reporters and everything else. This is what the book really is about.

Our ideas about what language is or should be do not have to be consistent or uniform. When we are growing up, we meet many contradictory messages. Parents say we should avoid slang and swearing, but we still hear *them* use it. Kids in the street or on the football field appreciate slang and swearing, as do our classmates at school. Teachers disapprove of it.

It is a reasonable guess that we learn our attitudes to language from the same sources or groups as teach us the use of language. These different ideas about language form the basis of situational variation in language. We learn how we should express ourselves in different situations if we want to be accepted.

This is not only an issue for young people. Grown-ups try to find the 'right' tone or style in most things they do – in giving a speech, writing a business letter or asking for a favour.

It is not easy to please all the people all the time. But many try. There are, however, a few very notable exceptions. The 'punk' ideology (and probably the ideology of other groups of youths) seems to say: try to please your own group by being offensive to everyone else.

FLU OR RIPE APPLE?

As youngsters or grown-ups we acquire new words, new pronunciations of old words, new meanings of old words and new grammatical constructions. How is this done? Are we innocent and defenceless victims of new trends in language or do we consciously and voluntarily pick up the neologisms presented to us? Do we catch the flu or do we steal a ripe apple from the neighbour's garden?

Take the word *yuppie*, for example. It appeared for the first time in the United States, some time during the 1980s. Is it the case that we started using this word as soon as we had heard it a couple of times? This is what the 'flu theory' suggests. Or did we hear the word, consider it, evaluate it and finally reach a decision as to whether we should use it? This is what the 'ripe apple theory' would suggest.

We think this is an important but also very hard question to answer. At the bottom of it we find the role of attitudes and free will in language change. It is surprising how little this question has been discussed or considered in linguistics. We do not have an answer to it but we do have some views.

Our best guess is that both theories have some truth in them. We are also confident that the role of free will and personal considerations is greater for the adult than for the child. Small children learn the language spoken around them and will probably learn most from the ones they talk with the most.

When we get older and more secure in our own language, more is needed to change it. Linguistically (and some people claim also politically) we become more conservative as the years pass by. As a rule adults probably learn the words, pronunciation and constructions that they want to learn, i.e. they pick up and follow the innovations they find necessary, reasonable, clever, witty and/or impressive. However, we do not want to rule out the possibility that a new word may slip into our active vocabulary against our will. And we certainly do not want to rule out the possibility of a new item entering our language without our noticing it.

In many cases, when a person moves from Britain to the United States, or vice versa, that person's accent changes a few steps between British and American English. For many millions of people who use English as a second language, it is quite clear that their English accent changes depending on who they communicate with. You can almost hear their accent travel across the Atlantic.

There are two reasons for discussing this question of flu or ripe apple. First of all, it is a neglected area of linguistic research. It is a question of real linguistic importance to investigate how much attitudes to language infuence language change. If it is the case, as we believe, that an individual's usage and changes in usage to a great extent are controlled by the individual's attitudes to language, then there are very good reasons to give these attitudes more consideration within the study of language. The study of these attitudes, linguistic ideologies, and even what we call bad language, may in fact be central rather than peripheral to many linguistic questions.

There is a noticeable difference in how professional linguists and ordinary people view questions of bad language and linguistic attitudes in general. When ordinary people discuss language, these issues play a central role and take up a lot of time. In linguistics they are much more peripheral and little time is spent on them. Maybe it is time for professional linguists to discuss these questions a bit more seriously.

The second reason for discussing this question has to do with the danger of so-called bad language. Some children read books that use 'good' language and some read books that use 'bad' language – all these judgements are made by the adult world, of course. Does this lead to a difference in quality between the language of these two groups? Many parents and teachers believe that this is the case. The stronger you believe in the 'flu theory', the greater you will perceive this danger to be.

Another favourite issue of this debate concerns the use of swearing, slang and other types of bad language in the mass media. Can these language phenomena really be so contagious that one or two swear-words on TV can lead youngsters to swear themselves? Allow us to doubt this. We find it hard to believe that one or two swearers out of the hundreds of people appearing on TV can seduce a child into using swear-words, unless the child really wants to pick the forbidden fruit, taste it and test it. And, if the child's parents are strongly against this type of language, this test will surely be a great success, especially if conducted in the presence of aunts, uncles and grandparents. No words come close to creating the same effect. There may be punishment afterwards, but the looks on the faces of the family make it almost worthwhile.

The point of this section has been to make clear not only that language is acquired at an early stage of life, but also that along with it comes a whole series of attitudes and views about language. A person's use of language is a product both of the language and of the attitudes to language that they have acquired through the years.

Do it!

Between 1980 and 1985 cars and signposts were often furnished with messages such as the following.

Bankers do it with interest.
Wind surfers do it standing up.
Make it legal. Do it with a lawyer.
Photographers do it in the dark.
Divers do it deeper.
Marathoners do it for hours.

Good or bad? Poison or spice in the language? Views are divided. Some dislike it because of the sexual content. Some like it because of its creativity. Whatever your views are: it has a sexual content and it is creative.

3

SWEARING

S WEARING IS 'BAD LANGUAGE'. There is no question about it. If ordinary people are asked 'What do you think of when you hear the phrase *bad language*?', most of them will certainly say 'swearing'.

It is much harder to define what swearing really is. Since swearing is more or less universal, we have to try to give it a general characterization and not just an English-specific one. We suggest that swearing can be defined as a type of language use in which the expression

(a) refers to something that is taboo and/or stigmatized in the culture;
(b) should not be interpreted literally;
(c) can be used to express strong emotions and attitudes.

To see how the definition works, we can look at the word *shit*. It literally refers to a tabooed item, namely excrement. However, when it is used for swearing, it is not meant in the literal sense, but instead in an emotive sense. By freeing the term, so to speak, from its referential duties, we can use it to express emotions and attitudes.

It is obvious that swearing can be used to show strong emotions. When your favourite football team is one goal behind and misses a penalty kick in the last minute of the game, there is no limit to the strength, volume and intensity of your *Damn it!* or whatever alternative expression you use. However, swearing does not have to be 'emotional'. In the following lines from David Storey's play *The Changing Room,* there are nine uses of the word *bloody.* If these were pronounced with the same force as *Damn it!* above, it would be difficult to deliver the lines or to listen to them.

Swearing

When swearing occurs with this kind of frequency, it is used as a 'style-giver'.

MORLEY (*off*). Any more for any more?
    (*Laughter off*.)
WALSH (*off*). Barry ...y! *We're waiting, Barry!*
FENCHURCH. Take no notice. Silly sod.
STRINGER. Where's Cliff, then?
JAGGER. Up in the directors' bath, old lad.
STRINGER. Is that right, then?
CROSBY. Captain's privilege, lad.
STRINGER. Bloody hell ... (*Snatches towel, goes over to the bench to dry himself.*)
    (LUKE *is still going round, dabbing on antiseptic.*)
LUKE. Any cuts, bruises: ought that needs fastening up?
JAGGER. I've a couple of things here that need a bit of bloody attention, Lukey ...
LUKE. What's that?
    (*Goes over;* JAGGER *shows him.*
    They all laugh.
    PATSY *has crossed to the mirror to comb his hair.*)
PATSY. Did you see a young woman waiting for me up there, Danny?
    (*Groans and jeers from the players.*)
CLEGG. How do you do it, Patsy? I can never make that out.
FENCHURCH. Nay, his girl-friend's a bloody schoolmistress. Isn't that right, then, Patsy?
    (PATSY *doesn't answer: combs his hair, straightens his tie.*)
JAGGER. Schoolmistress?
FENCHURCH. Teaches in Trevor's bloody school ... Isn't that right, then, Trev?
    (TREVOR *nods, doesn't look up: gets on with his dressing.*)
JAGGER. What do you talk about, then, Patsy?

> (*They laugh.* PATSY *is crossing to his coat. With some
> care he pulls it on.*)
> CLEGG (*having gone to him*). The moon in *June* ... Is coming
> out quite *soon!*

A typical form of swearing in English and most other European languages involves *blasphemic* utterances – that is, words which refer to (Christian) religion in a disrespectful way. We swear by heaven and hell and their inhabitants. Other swear-words, such as *piss off, cunt* and *sod*, come from two other areas from which many swear-words in many languages are taken – bodily functions and sex. The word *sod* as in *You sod!* and *Sod off!* is based on the word *sodomy* meaning homosexuality. So, even though the story of Sodom and Gomorrah has a religious source, *sod* is not an example of blasphemic swearing.

We shall now outline a general model of swearing. This model should be used as a tool for understanding what swearing is and how it could be studied. It includes the following five levels:

1 Taboo behaviour
2 Taboo words
3 Swear-words
4 Grammar of swearing
5 Social restrictions on swearing

TABOO BEHAVIOUR AND TABOO WORDS

There are things we are not supposed to do and there are words we are not supposed to say. Incest is taboo and so are words like *motherfucker*. This much is obvious. But anthropologists such as Lévi-Strauss, Edmund Leach and Mary Douglas have shown how taboos of different sorts are not just isolated facts in a culture but important elements in the structure and social life of a culture. In Western societies, we have taboos relating to sex, religion, bodily functions, ethnic groups, food, dirt and death. To say that a certain area of life is taboo is not to say that it is altogether forbidden,

---

The second commandment

Thou shalt not take the name of the LORD *thy God in vain; for the* LORD *will not hold him guiltless that taketh his name in vain.*

Exodus 20:7

The Bible prescribes serious or even capital punishment for swearing and cursing.

And he that curseth his father, or his mother, shall surely be put to death.

Exodus 21:17

And he that blasphemeth the name of the LORD, *he shall surely be put to death, and all the congregation shall certainly stone him: as well the stranger, as he that is born in the land, when he blasphemeth the name of the* LORD, *shall be put to death.*

Leviticus 24:16

---

out that it is regulated by conscious or unconscious rules. It is certainly not forbidden or improper to have sex, given the right time, place, person and maybe even the right motivation. The partner should be fairly close in many cultures (a certain class, group, colour, etc.) but not too close (incest), and should definitely be a human being (not an animal – bestiality).

Next, think about some 'unmentionable' bodily functions. These activities are certainly not forbidden. On the contrary, they are absolutely necessary for survival, but there are certain appropriate hidden places for them. Likewise, we don't talk about them. If we are forced to mention them, we have to obey the rules and choose the proper expressions (*urine* and *faeces* rather than *piss* and *shit*).

Note first, however, that there is great variation in what is taboo or significant in different cultures, and, second, that this can show up in different ways – as prohibition, obligation, or strict regulation. We expect swearing to be related to the areas which are taboo or significant in a particular culture. In Catholic and Orthodox countries, we find many more expressions relating to the Virgin Mary than in Protestant countries, for instance.

The relationship between taboo behaviour and taboo words can be a problem. It is tempting to look at this very simply and to suggest that, for every behavioural taboo, there will be a taboo word. However, this simple description seems to be false. Some taboo behaviours have corresponding taboo words; others do not. And sometimes taboo words *give rise to* taboo behaviours:

> It is not the case that certain kinds of behaviour are taboo
> and that, therefore, the language relating such behavior
> becomes taboo. Sometimes words may be taboo in themselves
> for linguistic (phonetic) reasons, and the causal link, if any,
> is then reversed: a behavioral taboo comes to reflect a prior
> verbal taboo.
>
> E. Leach, 'Anthropological aspects of language'

There are some very clear examples of purely linguistic taboos. In the Tiwi culture on the islands just north of Australia, as in other cultures in that area, the proper name of a dead person is taboo. But that is not all: words that sound like these proper names also become taboo. These words are thus taboo for linguistic reasons. An English example might be *ass*, referring to the animal – most people feel more comfortable with the word *donkey*, because of the linguistic similarity to *arse* (British)/*ass* (North American).

Mary Haas has given some examples of purely linguistic taboos among Thai-speakers in an English environment. They didn't use certain Thai words, because they sounded like obscene words in English. These words include *fâg*, 'sheath'; *fág*, 'to hatch'; *phríg*, '(chilli) pepper'; *chíd*, 'to be close, near'; and *khán* 'to crush', squeeze out'. The problem, of course, also exists in reverse. Thai-speakers avoided the perfectly normal English word *yet* because it sounded too close to Thai *jéd*, 'to have sexual intercourse'.

Are there behavioural taboos which don't have any corresponding taboo words? This question is much harder to answer and depends very much on what we mean by taboo words. Cannibalism is an obvious taboo behaviour in Europe. But, to our knowledge, there are no unprintable words in English referring to cannibalism, and we are certainly allowed to talk and write about cannibalism in distant cultures. It seems then that there are no corresponding taboo words. But what would happen if cannibalism, or even just signs of it, came close to us? Would we talk about it freely then?

Compare how we talk about the death of other people. We may talk about it freely when it is distant, but when it comes close to our own family we may feel a need to use all the euphemisms supplied by the language. This, of course, shows that there is some sort of linguistic taboo attached to death in our culture. As a general point, we may add that euphemisms as well as swear-words indicate underlying taboos.

SWEAR-WORDS

It is often said that swearing in Germanic languages such as English uses only a handful of words. It may be true that only a few taboo concepts or words are used, but these can be combined with other words and used in fixed expressions to make up a fairly elaborate system of swearing. For example, words for faeces are typical swear-words in European languages: *shit* (English), *Scheisse* (German), *skit* (Swedish), *merde* (French), *mierda* (Spanish), and so on. In German and Swedish this word can also be used as a prefix – that is, as the first part of a complex word. So we find words like *scheisseschlecht* and *skitdåligt* (literally 'shit bad') with a negative meaning, but also *scheissgut* and *skitbra* (literally 'shit good') with a positive meaning. As for fixed expressions, the phrase

Go to hell is a set and ready-made formula. We cannot substitute another verb of motion (such as *walk, run, jump*) for *go* in the phrase. So, when we talk about the vocabulary of swearing, we must include not only simple swear-words (*hell, fuck,* etc.) but also compound words (*skitbra*), formulas (*Go to hell*) and frames (*Who gives a ——?*). This is absolutely necessary if we want to end up with a correct description of the linguistic knowledge of a swearer.

When we use words like *shit* and phrases like *Go to hell* as swear-words, the literal meaning is very distant. We may call this relationship between the literal meaning and derived meaning a type of metaphor, mainly because there is no better term available, but we feel uneasy about using this term. We must remember that these really are cases of 'long-distance' metaphors. It is obvious that the use and meaning of these phrases have been extended and that the literal meaning has faded away or been completely lost. The simple fact that the following three expressions, whose literal meanings are quite different, may have the same function in an appropriate situation (to get someone to leave) proves this point:

> *Go to hell!*
> *Fuck off!*
> *Get your ass out of here!*

The meaning of these and similar expressions is easiest to describe in terms of their function in specific situations – literal meaning does not take us very far. Furthermore, these words and formulas can be used in some situations but not in others. Some can express anger, some surprise, some agreement, and so on.

The definition of swearing presented at the beginning of the chapter certainly does not limit the scope of swearing to expletives – that is, to swearing used to express emotions. We can widen the horizon and look at a much larger set of expressions. There are other uses of swearing, but unfortunately it is rather hard to come

Variations on a popular theme

Perhaps one of the most interesting and colourful words in the English language today is *fuck*. It can be used to describe pain, pleasure, hate and, last but not least, love. Besides its sexual connotation, this word can be utilized to describe many situations:

FRAUD	I got fucked by my insurance agent.
DISMAY	Oh, fuck it!
TROUBLE	I guess I'm fucked now.
AGGRESSION	Fuck you!
PASSIVE	Fuck me.
CONFUSION	What the fuck?
DIFFICULTY	I can't understand this fucking business.
DESPAIR	Fucked again.
PHILOSOPHICAL	Who gives a fuck.
INCOMPETENCE	He's all fucked up.
LAZINESS	He's a fuck-off.
DISPLEASURE	What the fuck is going on?
REBELLION	Oh, fuck-off!

(The source of this non-authorized study of a verb with many uses is completely unknown to us.)

up with a useful characterization of types of swearing. However, let us try.

EXPLETIVE

Used to express emotions; not directed towards others.
>   Examples: *Hell!*, *Shit!*, *God damn it!*

ABUSIVE

Directed towards others; derogatory; includes name-calling and different types of curses.
>   Examples: *You asshole!*, *You bastard!*, *Go to hell!*

Apart from these two major types, we can find a number of secondary uses of swearing:

HUMOROUS

Directed towards others but not derogatory; often takes the form of abusive swearing but has the opposite function; is playful rather than offensive.
>   Example: *Get your ass in gear!*

AUXILIARY

Not directed towards a person or situation; swearing, as a way of speaking ('lazy swearing'); often or always non-emphatic.
>   Examples: *this fucking X, bloody Y.*

GRAMMAR OF SWEARING

To a large extent this is straightforward. The ordinary rules of the grammar taken together with the vocabulary of swearing give us grammatical swearing in that language.

An example of a grammatical rule that applies specifically to swearing involves additions of swear-words or euphemisms to question-words in several European languages from different language families:

> *Who the hell has been here?*

> *Vem i helvete har varit här?* (Swedish)
> Who in hell has been here?

> *Co za cholera tu byla?* (Polish)
> Who for cholera here was?

> *Ki a fene volt itt?* (Hungarian)
> Who the sickness was here?

Notice that in English it is ungrammatical to say 'Who *in* hell has been here?' The gut reaction of many native speakers is of course that anything that includes swearing is incorrect, but this shows that there is a distinction between being grammatically correct and being socially correct. There are, of course, other grammatical rules that are specific to swearing. On the whole, however, the grammar is the same for swearing as for ordinary language.

On the other hand, there may be differences between languages in the degree to which swearing can intrude into the grammatical patterns of the language. One theory gives the following five levels of interruption (1 is the top level). There are two implicational hierarchies connected with these levels. First, if a language has swearing on one level, it will have swearing on all levels above this. Second, if a language has a certain number of possibilities (e.g. in terms of words and phrases available) of swearing on one level, it will have a greater number of possibilities on all the levels above this.

Swear-words may intrude into grammatical patterns

1 as separate utterances (expletives and abusives):
   Shit! Jesus Christ! You Bastard! God damn you!

2 as 'adsentences' (loosely tied to a sentence, before or after):
   Shit, I forgot all about it.
   You have to tell me, for God's sake!

3 as major constituents of a sentence (subject, verb, adverb, etc.):

That stupid bastard came to see me.
He fucks up everything.
He managed – God damn it – to get his degree.

4 as part of a constituent of a sentence (adjective, adverb):

this fucking train
a bloody big house

5 as part of a word (compound or derivational, as prefix, suffix or infix):

skitbra (shit good)
bilhelvetet (car hell)
Tenne-goddam-see
abso-bloody-lutely

SOCIAL RESTRICTIONS ON SWEARING

It is an extremely hard task to compare the frequency of swearing in different cultures. No one can really be expected to have a complete knowledge of swearing even in the various layers of their own society. Even within one culture there seem to be differences in the frequency of swearing between different groups and within one and the same group. Still, there is no need to give up the search for descriptions and explanations of these differences, as long as the difficulties are kept in mind. We shall present a theory below which tries to explain such differences.

We have found that, when people are asked about arguments for or against swearing, the religious, moral, social and aesthetic arguments take a back seat to linguistic arguments. For example, a popular explanation for swearing is that swear-words are words you use when you have no others at your disposal. This argument sees swearing as a personal weakness – your vocabulary is so small that you have to use these 'easy' and 'lazy' words. This linguistic (or 'pseudo-linguistic') case against swearing is very common. Interestingly enough, the most common argument in favour of swearing is an identical one – that swear-words are words you use when you have no others at your disposal. But in this case swearing is not seen as a personal weakness. Instead, the argument says that there are certain situations in which no other words would be appropriate.

Explanations can, however, be found that reach beyond such popular and superficial arguments. Swearing is tied to social restrictions which mirror the values of the society. These restrictions are important parts of the structure of the society, not merely historical accidents, and can be very deep-seated. In her book *Natural Symbols,* Mary Douglas presents an elegant line of reasoning which relates social behaviour to social structure and values:

> I here argue that a social structure which requires a high
> degree of conscious control will find its style at a high level
> of formality, stern application of the purity rule, denigration
> of organic process and wariness towards experiences in
> which control of consciousness is lost.

The *purity rule* is a general principle with several applications. The extent to which people follow the purity rule will show up in how clean, tidy and orderly they keep their homes, gardens, desks, hair, clothes, and so on. We could certainly add their use of language to this list, since swearing is no doubt a good example of the 'untidy' use of language. The strength of this reasoning hinges on the possibility of grouping these different areas of behaviour together. Order in one place implies order in other places. Order in life implies order in language.

It is important to realize that these concepts are relative to the culture we live in. A nice illustration of this is given by our desire to keep our clothes clean. It has been shown that a family today spends about the same amount of time washing clothes as a family did a hundred years ago. On the other hand, technical developments have given us washing machines which reduce washing time enormously. The result is, of course, that we keep our clothes much cleaner today. The socially relevant point, however, continues to be how clean we keep them in relation to other members of the society.

Mary Douglas relates her theory about tne general concept of purity to Basil Bernstein's theory of (linguistic) socialization. According to Bernstein, some families have a positional role structure while others have a personal role structure. Douglas applies this distinction to society as a whole. A positional role society would be a strictly ordered society where each person's position in the structure determines their rights and duties. A personal-role society would be a society where the individual's abilities and ambitions are important in deciding their future career and thus their rights and duties.

This theory predicts that we should expect to find differences in swearing both between different societies and between different members of the same society. Assuming that swearing is language that is 'untidy', informal and/or typical of loss of control, let us look more closely at how this works.

At the most general level, we would expect societies with a high degree of conscious control or a positional role structure to have less swearing than societies with less conscious control or a personal role structure. Victorian England leaned more towards positional roles and conscious control than today's England, so we would guess that swearing has increased since the days of Queen Victoria. This is probably true (although we don't have statistical evidence), at least as long as we look only at those groups in the society that were true to the Victorian values. The theory doesn't apply to outsiders.

At the next level, we expect that different groups or layers of society will have different social values. Because of this, we can look for separate groups to vary in their social behaviour, for example in their use of swearing. At the individual level, people who are cornerstones in the social structure are expected to keep their appearance and language pure and clean. Individuals on the edges of society – young people, the unemployed, alcoholics and criminals (with the most peripheral last) – can be expected to show less control over their social behaviour and language. And there is no doubt that swearing is very typical of peripheral groups.

RITUAL SWEARING

There is also a type of ritualized swearing in many speech communities in the world, notably in American black communities, where it is referred to as *sounding, signifying* or *playing the dozens.* If it is characterized as a type of swearing, it could be said to be both humorous and abusive. But to a large extent the abusiveness is due to the literal meaning of the taboo words. Hence, it is more insulting than swearing.

Two examples from William Labov's book *Language in the Inner City:*

> *I don't play the dozens, the dozens ain't my game*
> *But the way I fucked your mama is a god damn shame.*

> *I hate to talk about your mother, she's a good old soul*
> *She got a ten-ton pussy and a rubber asshole.*

We can even go one step further and look at the individual in different situations. Usually we say that swearing is more frequent in informal situations than in formal ones. When the President gives a speech to the nation, we have an extremely formal situation, and we certainly expect 'proper' and 'decent' language to be used. However, if he is chatting to his close friends over a few drinks, we have a much more informal situation, and this will have noticeable effects on the language used.

4

SLANG

THERE IS NO good definition of slang available in the literature. The linguist Paul Roberts said that slang was 'one of those things that everybody can recognize and nobody can define'. This is a realistic characterization, but there are also several more colourful ones. The American poet Carl Sandburg said that 'Slang is a language that rolls up its sleeves, spits on its hands, and goes to work.' G. K. Chesterton, the English novelist, said even more admirably that 'The one stream of poetry which is constantly flowing is slang. Every day some nameless poet weaves some fairy tracery of popular language ... All slang is metaphor, and all metaphor is poetry.'

The most important aspect of slang it that it is language use below the level of stylistically neutral language usage. The concept of stylistically neutral language is not well defined, and what is below this level must therefore also be vague. But it is below this level that we find an extensive stylistic scale ranging from colloquial to vulgar and obscene. As we use the term *slang*, it refers to colloquial as well as vulgar language.

This leaves us with slang as a rather wide concept. Instead of attempting to define it, however, we will try to characterize slang by stating what it is and what it is not. We begin by repeating ourselves.

SLANG IS LANGUAGE USE BELOW THE NEUTRAL STYLISTIC LEVEL

This statement is admittedly vague, but it makes the necessary point that slang is a relative concept. Since slang is relative, changes in neutral or formal usage will lead to changes in what is seen as slang. Many people have a feeling that the stylistic level of the mass media has fallen. Journalists do not speak and write as 'properly' as they used to, they say. If this is true, and to some extent and in certain areas we believe it to be true (grammatical constructions are not as elaborate as before, for example), this could mean that words and phrases that used to be slang are now considered to be part of neutral or 'proper' language.

If you know a little French, you'll know that *tête* means 'head'. This is a normal, ordinary and neutral word in standard French. If, however, you follow this word back in history, you will find its roots in Latin *testa*, which meant 'pot', 'bowl'. Thus *tête* was originally a slang term, but has subsequently made it into the standard language. Compare this to the English word *blockhead*, which was slang in the sixteenth century and still is. Of course, there are English slang words which moved from slang into neutral or even formal language. *Phone*, *bike*, *bus* and *pub* once were slangy versions of the more 'proper' *telephone*, *bicycle*, *omnibus* and *public house*. *Dove* and *hawk* as political and/or military terms were once slang. Few people think of them as that today. The moral of the story is evident. Slang changes through time. What is slang for one person, generation or situation may not be slang for another.

However, this is not the only direction in which changes take place, especially for individuals. Suppose you move, by education, marriage or whatever, from one layer of society to another. You may find that what you previously considered neutral language is now viewed as slang. Long before Eliza Doolittle met Professor Higgins, she could tell proper language from slang. So could Professor Higgins, of course. She later learned that the dividing line between the two types of language use was drawn at a different place by the professor.

It is also true that what is slang may vary from place to place, dialect to dialect. *Lad* and *lass* may be slang for some speakers of English. For others they are simply neutral, plain language and nothing else. In the north of England, *lad* is a neutral stylistic expression, as in *I've got two lads*, meaning, 'I have two sons'. However, in the south *lad* is a slang term, as in *He's one of the lads* meaning 'He is one of the gang' (used about adult male persons).

SLANG IS TYPICAL OF INFORMAL SITUATIONS

This is rather self-evident. The formality of language, as we saw in Chapter 3, is tied to the situation: in a formal situation we expect formal language and in an informal situation informal language. Slang is far more out of place or shocking at the Queen's dinner table than in the locker-room.

The formality of a situation is not fixed once and for all, but its changes through time and from one place to another. The relationship between student and professor is an example of one such situation. As far as we can judge from our experience, this situation is more formal in Britain than in the United States. But in both places this situation has become less formal since the late 1960s. (There are a few lasting results of the student revolts in 1968!)

However, there is no simple or automatic relationship between the formality of the situation and language. Usually both change together, and very often this goes unnoticed. During the first minutes or hours of a new relationship, the situation is usually felt to be somewhat formal. After a while it loosens up and the language becomes less formal.

The effects are certainly noticeable if the formality of the language changes without there being a corresponding change in the formality of the situation. In the sociolinguistic literature this has been called a *metaphorical shift*. It can occur for a number of reasons and have many different effects. Suppose, for example, that you have worked for an employer for about half a year and you have talked with your boss a couple of times every week in a rather normal and formal way. Then, one day, your employer for no special reason uses a more 'sloppy' kind of language, with slang, swearing and similar things in the conversation. Our guess is that you would notice this change of stylistic level and that you would interpret it as a friendly gesture, even as a sign of respect. This may sound paradoxical, but the truth is that the language used between equals or near-equals (some people will always be more equal than others) tends to be less formal. So, when your boss swears with you, you have advanced in the company. When he swears at you, it is the other way around.

SLANG IS TYPICAL OF SPOKEN LANGUAGE

This is more or less a consequence of the previous point about the formality of the language and the situation. Most people are both speakers and writers – at least, writers of postcards and shopping lists. On the whole and for most of us, the situations in which we write are more formal than the situations in which we talk. Think about such things as applying for a building permit or a tax deduction – slang rarely occurs in this kind of writing. There are counter-examples, of course. Giving a speech at a wedding party is certainly viewed as a more formal situation than leaving a note for the next-door neighbour.

If you go and watch a football game, you will no doubt hear a lot of slang from the crowd around you. The next morning when you read about the match in the newspaper, there will be far less slang in the paper's coverage of the game, we promise you.

The language of mass media – newspapers, radio and TV broadcasting – contains very little slang. There is, however, one type of written material which contains quite a lot of slang – novels and short stories, especially their dialogues. An important way for an author to show what the characters are like is through their language. In such contexts, the characterizations are more important than the formality expected in written language.

SLANG IS FOUND IN WORDS, NOT IN GRAMMAR

When people talk about slang, they usually mean words, not grammar or pronunciation. This is more or less the correct view. Still, we often talk about 'slang language', which is not accurate. Every language contains both a vocabulary and a grammar. English is a language but slang is not. Likewise, it is linguistically incorrect to talk about the 'language' of students, lawyers, thieves and so on. However, here and there in the book we shall talk about language in this technically incorrect way. There are not many alternative expressions to use.

There are dozens of slang dictionaries for the English language. But there is not one single grammar of English slang. Could there be such a grammar? Probably not. There are perhaps a handful of features which could be regarded as typical of slang grammar, but there are very few compared to the enormous number of words belonging to slang. Hence, slang is first and foremost a question of vocabulary.

SLANG IS NOT DIALECT

When we talk about slang in this book, we talk about it as a general phenomenon common to the whole language community. We can talk about English slang and French slang. Sometimes British, American and Australian slang are seen as separate even though the common language (English) is almost the same.

Dialects are restricted to one region or social class within the language community. This is not *necessarily* the case with slang. Of course, there are differences in slang between different localities. There are many regional and social differences in slang. Some slang items, such as *whistle* (suit) in Cockney, are restricted to a regional dialect, while others are confined to a social class: *tosh* (nonsense), for instance, is probably mostly used by upper-class people. Other slang items, such as *knackered* (tired) in Britain, can be found in all regions. We shall discuss this further in the chapter on education.

As we said above, slang is language use below the level of neutral language usage. For someone growing up in a dialect-speaking area, there is a clear difference between the ordinary, neutral and proper language used on most occasions and the slang you may use with friends and on special occasions. Stylistic variation, including the use of slang, can take place *within* dialects.

73

This should be rather obvious. Local politicians can certainly give speeches in the local dialect. Maybe they are even better off doing that. They should not give a speech containing slang, however – at least not if they are looking for support from school-teachers, farmers and grandmothers, who may be all in favour of the dialect but who may not like slang at all.

People who are raised in a social setting where they do not use local dialect may mistakenly confuse dialect and slang. For them both slang and dialect are examples of 'non-standard' language use.

The situation can cause problems at school. Teachers often discuss which words and constructions should be allowed at school. It is not always easy to see where to draw the line between standard language, dialect, slang and mistakes. We discuss this further in chapter 9.

SLANG IS NOT SWEARING

Swearing, as we said in the previous chapter, is always connected with taboos of some kind. Slang terms are not restricted in such a way.

Many English swearing expressions are taken from the areas of sex and bodily functions. It is also the case that there are quite a few slang terms of relating to these areas. To prove the point, we give a list of some of synonyms for *urinate* and *defecate* (from Spears, *Slang and Euphemism*, 1982).

Urinate   Answer nature's call, bog, burn the grass, check the ski rack, coke-stop, drain the spuds, find a haven of rest, give the china-man a music lesson, go and catch a horse, go and look at the crops, go and see if the horse has kicked off his blanket, go to Egypt, pay a visit, pluck a rose, post a letter, powder one's nose, retire, see a man about a dog/horse, see Johnny, see Mrs Murphy, visit the sand-box, wash, wash one's hands, wash up.

Defecate   Alvum exonerare, big hit, BM, bury a Quaker, ca-ca, capoop, cast, chuck a turd, clart, cuck, deposit, dispatch one's cargo, do a job, drop one's load, drop one's wax, drop turds, dump, ease nature, ease oneself, evacuate the bowels, fill one's pants, George, go, go to the bathroom, grunt, hockey, Irish shave, job, make a deposit, perform the work of nature, pick a daisy, poop, poo-poo, post a letter, potty, quat, relieve oneself, rump, scumber, shit, siege, smell the place up, soil one's linen, squat, stook, take a crap, take a dump, take a shit, unfeed, void.

Similar lists for words relating to sexual activities and sex organs would be even more impressive (or offensive). But the point is that slang terminology also relates to completely innocent areas of content, such as sport, music, food and housing.

Since the days of the French linguist de Saussure, it has been customary to think of a word (or a *linguistic sign*, as he would call it), as a two-part unit of form and content. The word *house* would be illustrated as follows (the 'form' is phonetic).

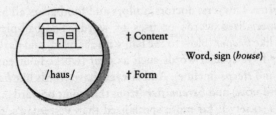

House is a neutral word. But other words, like slang and swearing, can arouse negative attitudes. These attitudes may be connected with the form and/or the content. By combining the expressions *neutral* and *bad* with form and content, we get four possibilities for characterizing words.

Word of types II and IV can be called slang. The important characteristic of slang is that the form is considered to be stylistically very informal. The content can be either neutral or taboo.

Swearing is a special use of type IV words in which these

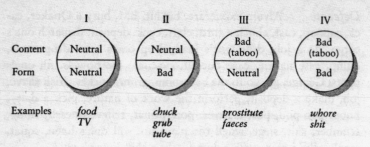

	I	II	III	IV
Content	Neutral	Neutral	Bad (taboo)	Bad (taboo)
Form	Neutral	Bad	Neutral	Bad
Examples	*food* *TV*	*chuck* *grub* *tube*	*prostitute* *faeces*	*whore* *shit*

words or phrases are used emotively and with a widened meaning. When *Shit!* is used in swearing, it does not literally refer to defecation, as was pointed out in the previous chapter. In slang, *shit* really means 'shit' (or 'faeces', if you prefer that term).

SLANG IS NOT REGISTER

Every occupation and activity has its own specialized vocabulary or *register*. Lawyers, doctors, sailors and footballers all have their own specialized words or uses of words. Football-players use words like *header* (blow to the ball with the head) and *park* (pitch). Miners have special words such as *goaf* (worked-out part of the mine) and *steeps* (incline). And lawyers have words like *heretofore* (up until now) and *hereinafter* (from this point onwards). Because today's society is far more specialized than yesterday's, there has been a great increase in the number of specialized vocabularies in society. This process of specialization, which still continues, is probably one of the most important factors in vocabulary development in the modern world. The only other force which competes in importance is the market-place, where so many new things are always on offer. The market does not just provide us with *trousers* but with many different types of trousers: *jeans*, *Bermudas*, *culottes*, *cords*, and so on and so forth. Most items need a name in order to sell.

Registers are not the same thing as slang, but they may *contain* slang, in so far as the specialized vocabulary is informal. Doctors, for instance, may say to patients that they will check their *reflexes*, but to a fellow doctor this may be reported as a check of the patients' *jerks*. The patient leaves a tissue sample for examination, but doctors may say that they are sending some *meat* to the laboratory. As a patient you may go to the X-ray department, but insiders may call it *sparks*. These words are not defined in books on medicine, but are learned and used in practice. In most types of work there is, within the register, both an official terminology and an unofficial terminology or specialized slang.

Registers associated with unofficial, peripheral or illegal activities may predominantly consist of slang. Consider the narcotics business, which unfortunately is an important factor in modern society. It is an industry which has a turnover bigger than that of many important companies and which involves very many people. It is a trade, however, which lies on the fringes of society. As a consequence, most of its register consists of slang, unlike the specialized vocabularies of doctors and lawyers, who work in the established sector of society. Interestingly, some narcotics terminology often finds its way out of this register and into general slang vocabulary – there may in fact be no other area of modern life which influences slang as much as the narcotics trade. Words such as *high*, *stoned*, *freaked out*, *turned on*, which have to do with the effects of drug abuse, seem frequently to find their way into general usage. On the other hand, terms for equipment such as *bhang* (water pipe) and *chillum* (pipe) seem to have remained within the specialist register, although *fix* (dose) is now used more generally in connection with non-narcotic substances such as chocolate and sunshine.

We discuss register further in chapter 9.

SLANG IS NOT CANT, ARGOT OR JARGON

Today slang is a broad concept including colloquialisms, informalities and vulgarities of many types. Originally the term *slang* was used by British criminals to refer to their own special language.

Cant was the word used by the outside world and it is still used as a term for the language of criminals. Thus, slang has, as a concept, moved a long way from its origin.

Argot is, just like cant, a name for the language of criminals. Its origin is French, where it has been used for several centuries with this meaning.

Jargon, as this term is widely used today, refers to the insider's specialized register as viewed by the (usually resentful) outsider (see also Chapter 9).

SLANG IS CREATIVE

The creative aspect of slang is important. The point of slang words is often to be startling, amusing or shocking. Something must be done to make them stand out against the other, more ordinary lexical items.

Words such as *a*, *an*, *the*, *and* and *but* are very common but pass more or less unnoticed. Although they are understood, of course, slang words such as *groovy*, *heavy*, and so on, attract attention. However, if these words are heard over and over again, they soon lose their impact. And, if they are used as frequently as *a* or *the* in a conversation, listening becomes a chore. Words like *heavy* and *groovy* are therefore worn out in a few years or so. Groups using them will then turn to other words. Of course, in the meantime these words may be accepted and incorporated into other groups' vocabularies. Popular slang words are spread in much the same way as other trends – they appear in London before you find them in Leeds, and in New York before Buffalo.

We shall come back to this creative aspect of slang shortly.

SLANG IS OFTEN SHORT-LIVED

Words such as *chum* and *chap* have been slang for a long time, but most slang words either make it into accepted neutral style or else die out rather quickly.

There are thousands of English slang words which have been

lost. Some of these have been recorded in word lists. Others never reached the word lists or any other written document. Most slang terms are local in both time and place. The short life of most slang terms is directly connected with the creativity of slang. The enormous numbers of new slang words constitute a threat to the old ones, which they often replace.

SLANG IS OFTEN CONSCIOUS

When speakers use slang words, they are often aware that they are doing so. When we speak, we concentrate on finding the right strategy for presenting the content we want to communicate. Words with primarily grammatical function come without effort – only foreigners worry about *a*, *an*, *the* and words like that. The important thing for the native speaker is to find the right words which will give precisely the intended meaning. Slang words, however, can be important for finding precision in expression, rather than in content.

The main reason for this is social. The language of a group functions as a kind of glue which maintains cohesion between the members of this group and acts as a wall between them and outsiders. By choosing the right words you show which group you belong to. You can probably even show that you are one of the core members of the group.

It has been said that one function of the language of thieves and drug addicts is to keep the content of their conversations secret – outsiders should not understand what is being said. This is sometimes called *anti-language*. Since, however, most of the words they use are not at all hard to understand, this claim is dubious. However, there are other ways to keep outsiders outside. A member of the narcotics police has informed us that the language of drug addicts changes rapidly, which makes it very hard for the police to train informers for infiltration into these groups. It is easy to learn the slang words, but it is hard to keep up to date and use and combine words correctly. In this way it is easy for the group members to tell who is a true member of the group.

Another reason for the conciousness behind the choice of slang words is, of course, the intention to be startling, amusing or shocking. Such effects are not reached without conscious effort.

SLANG IS GROUP-RELATED

It is not the case that each group has a unique type of slang. There may, as we have seen, be some items unique to a group, but most terms are taken from the great pool of general slang terminology.

It is true, though, that different groups make different use of slang. Slang terms are not all equal. Some are more slangy or vulgar than others. Different groups use slang at different stylistic levels. Among a group of members of Parliament, even rather weak slang words may be used with some kind of audible quotation marks around them: *this 'hm-heavy' movie.*

Some social groups, moreover, use more slang than others. Most people think that teenagers are the prime users of slang, but this is hard to verify. According to one American investigation carried out by Willand Gore at Michigan University in 1896, students claimed that they used slang most when they were between sixteen and nineteen. However, it is not correct to regard slang as some kind of adolescent linguistic disease. Adults use a lot of slang, but, of course, there are differences between individuals as well as groups, depending on sex, social class and type of work. In this respect slang is no different from other types of 'bad language'.

SLANG IS ANCIENT

Aristophanes, who died in 385 BC, is usually said to have been the first writer who used slang extensively. His comedies feature many common people in good spirits using slang. Among the Roman writers, Plautus, Horace, Juvenal and Petronius are often mentioned as authors who knew how to use slang for stylistic purposes.

Of course, it is hard to judge what is slang and what is not when we look at foreign languages far back in time. In order to grasp which expressions are slang, we need a fairly good knowledge of the language. We are best at evaluating our own language today.

However, most speakers of English have little difficulty in recognizing at least some of the slang in Shakespeare. Here are a few examples from Shakespeare's plays. The list could be made very long.

board	(to) address	*dry*	dull
kickshaw (quelque chose)	trifle	*praise*	(to) appraise
tester, testril	sixpence	*tend*	(to) attend
clod-pole	blockhead	*clay-brained*	stupid

The examples are taken from Eric Partridge's book *Slang Today and Yesterday*. The book shows that there is an enormous amount of slang to be found in English literature from past centuries. Shakespeare was by no means the only writer who used slang and colloquial language in his writings.

WHERE DOES SLANG COME FROM?

Words circulate in the language. Many old slang words are accepted and taken into the neutral styles. After a generation or two, there is nothing slangy left in them. Sometimes they may pass from slang to neutral language through an intermediate state of being vogue words. By *vogue words* we mean words and phrases which become popular and very frequent for a short period of time.

Vogue words share two important characteristics with slang terms. First, they become very popular and frequent for a short period of time, a couple of years or so. Secondly, they receive a wider meaning or function than the ordinary usage of the word.

Look at *hot*, for example. We know the original meaning of *hot*. As a slang or vogue word it means far more than 'having a high temperature'. In slang *hot* can mean things like 'urgent', 'wanted by the police, 'stolen', 'performing well', 'angry', 'sexy' and 'popular'. As a vogue word, it is most common in the first and last senses: 'urgent', as in a *hot line* between Washington and Moscow or discussing a *hot potato*; and 'popular' as in a *hot* record, movie or performer.

We can illustrate the circulation of words with a simple diagram.

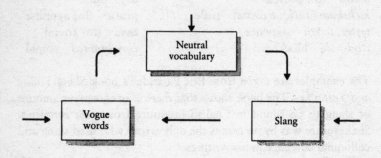

In this figure, we see how words can get out of the slang box. The next issue is how they got in there. Were do we get our slang words from? We suggest that the language acquires slang terms in three principal ways: new expressions are invented; old standard language expressions appear in new uses; and expressions are borrowed from one language or type of language by another. Under these three headings, there are different subtypes. We admit that it is sometimes rather hard to draw the line between them.

INVENTING NEW EXPRESSIONS

WORDS

goof   to blunder
freak out   lose control, be unable to cope with
dum-dum   idiot
yuppie   young, upwardly mobile professional

PHRASES

wooden overcoat   coffin
no dice   impossible
kick the bucket   die
on the hill   pregnant
dead duck   complete failure

CHANGING OLD EXPRESSIONS

NEW USES

juice   to bribe
fox   girl
high, stoned   intoxicated

NEW FORMS

yob   boy
kool toul   look out
Kate and Sidney   steak and kidney

Of these, *yob* and *kool toul* are backslang. *Kate and Sidney* is a type of rhyming slang.

SHORTENED FORMS

newsie   newspaper seller
fan   fanatic
narc   narcotics agent
hubbie   husband
geri   geriatric, old

Short forms are new forms of longer forms, of course.

BORROWING
DIRECT LOANS

nark   police informer (Romany *nak*, nose)

mush   face (Romany *moosh*, man)
gazlon   swindler (Yiddish *gozlin*, swindle)
fress   eat (Yiddish *fress*, eat)
pukka   genuine, honest (Hindi *pakka*, substantial)

LOAN TRANSLATION

It is not easy to find examples in English, because today English is a very successful loan-giver, while the other European languages are the loan-takers. There is an enormous surplus in the balance of trade for the English language – or, should we say, for the American English language.

Look at the following examples of loans from English narcotics slang into German, French and Swedish.

snow (heroin): Ger *Schnee*, Fr *neige*, Sw *snö*
stoned (intoxicated): Ger *stoned*, Fr *stone*, Sw *stenad/stoned*
fix (injection): Ger *Fix*, Fr *fixe*, Sw *fix*
horse (heroin): Ger *horse*, Fr *cheval*, Sw *häst*
high (intoxicated): Ger *high*, Fr *high*, Sw *hög*

It is interesting to note the variation between direct loans and loan translations. *Snow* regularly appears in translated forms. *Horse* is translated in French and Swedish but appears as a direct loan in German. In the case of *high*, Swedish translates the word but the other two languages do not. In many cases we find a slang term both in a direct loan form and as a loan translation.

THE CREATIVITY OF SLANG

As we said earlier, creativity is an essential aspect of slang, to a greater degree than with other types of language use. The use of slang is conscious, with the user being aware of the form of expression, as well as the content.

Many slang expressions – for example, *get one's ass in gear* (hurry up), *get to first base* (make headway), *dead from the neck up* (stupid), *the apple of one's eye* (one's favourite), – are meta-phorical in origin. The first time they are used they are truly creative. They attract attention and the speaker/inventor might be praised. When these phrases are used over and over again, their freshness is lost and they turn into rather ordinary lexical items. They are then often called *frozen metaphors*. This then creates a need for new expressions, new metaphors.

In a purely rational language, you might think that a principle like 'one concept – one word' would be the ideal. Human language is not like that, however, and slang will certainly never honour such a principle. Instead there is a constant desire to create new and dramatic expressions. Few words sound as old as do old slang terms. When teachers and parents try to speak the language of their pupils and children, they always make fools of themselves.

In ordinary language we have words living on through the generations without much change. Some of these have been in use as far back as we can trace the English language and other languages. *Foot, hand, arm, head, heart, star, sun, moon, earth, one, two, three,* and so on, belong to this category. These common words have counterparts which look very similar in the other Germanic or European language. These words are central to mankind, no matter where and how we live, unlike words such as *car, train, video recorder* and *astronaut*. Slang is rather different. It would be very unusual for a slang word to live on in the language for a thousand years or more. If it does, it will probably not be slang all that time.

In language there is both a core of words and expressions which are extremely stable and a large group of words which are more or less in flux. It is in this second part of the vocabulary where speakers can exercise their linguistic creativity by inventing new words, expressions and meanings.

Simple proof of the creativity of language can be gathered by any schoolteacher. If you ask each pupil to write down as many words as they can meaning, for example, 'boy', 'girl', 'good', 'bad' or 'stupid', you will get an amazing result. The number and variety of words will be immense. We are confident that if we gave this type of exercise every fifth year at the same school, we would see several new words introduced in the slang vocabulary every time.

Let us point out another relevant issue in this connection. As linguists we are often asked questions which may be very hard to answer, such as

Isn't it true that children today have smaller vocabularies than we did when we were young?
Children today use fewer synonyms than we did, don't they?

There are at least two ways to answer such questions. First, we can say that we just do not know and that it is impossible to know such things. We do not know how many words we knew when we were ten or fifteen. No one does. We do not know how many synonyms we have in our vocabulary today and we certainly do not know how many or which synonyms were there thirty years ago.

Secondly, we can answer these questions by referring to the list of words for 'stupid person' (see p. 87). Young people are not always short of words and they are obviously capable of learning synonyms. Adults may not always like the words young people use, but they are not short of words.

Besides, we have a feeling that our parents were not always impressed by our vocabulary and our choice of words when we were young. Things are much the same today as they have always been.

WHY SLANG?

The following fifteen reasons for using slang are taken from Eric Partridge, *Slang Today and Yesterday*.

1 *In sheer high spirits, by the young in heart as well as by the young in years; 'just for the fun of the thing'; in playfulness or waggishness.*

2 *As an exercise either in wit and ingenuity or in humour.*

3 *To be 'different', to be novel.*

4 *To be picturesque.*

5 *To be unmistakably arresting, even startling.*

6 *To escape from clichés, or to be brief and concise.*

7 *To enrich the language.*

8 *To lend an air of solidity, concreteness, to the abstract; of earthiness to the idealistic; of immediacy and appositeness to the remote.*

9a *To lessen the sting of, or on the other hand to give additional point to, a refusal, a rejection, a recantation.*

9b *To reduce, perhaps also disperse, the solemnity, the pomposity, the excessive seriousness of a conversation*

9c *To soften the tragedy, to lighten or to 'prettify' the inevitability of death or madness, or to mask the ugliness or the pity of profound turpitude.*

10 *To speak or write down to an inferior, or to amuse a superior public; or merely to be on a colloquial level with either one's audience or one's subject matter.*

11 *For ease of social intercourse.*

12 *To induce either friendliness or intimacy of a deep or a durable kind.*

13 *To show that one belongs to a certain school, trade, profession or social class; in brief, to be 'in the swim' or to establish contact.*

14 *Hence, to show or prove that someone is not 'in the swim'.*

15 *To be secret – not to be understood by those around one.*

WORDS FOR 'STUPID PERSON'

55 children aged 13–14 were asked to list expressions meaning 'stupid person'. Each of the following 129 words were produced by more than one child:

47	wally	dingo	dozy
40	stupid	dippo	duck
33	dimbo	dodo	Erny
	idiot	drip	Ernest
24	prat	headcase	featherbrain
23	dumbo	idiotic	flop head
21	dickhead	Johnny	freak
15	dippy	Nelly	goof
	dumb	nitwit	goofy
14	silly	nutcase	goon
	thicko	pranny	gooseberry
13	nerd	3 banana	hairy
12	dappy	diphead	halfwit
10	berk	div	imbecile
9	peabrain	dur brain	Joey
8	daft	fool	kipper
	nutter	gimp	knob
7	cabbage	knob end	lamebrain
	dim	Lenny	loony
	dimstick	nappy rash	Nancy
	dummy	numbskull	novice
	melon	pillock	nut
	square	Rodney	nutty
6	brainless	sawdust brain	oaf
	dopey	Scooby Doo	peanut brain
	flid	silly willy	pig
	jerk	spasmo	prathead
	mophead	squarehead	remmy
	spaz	thicky	sausage

thick head
5 cauliflower
dildo
divvy
dunce
lemon
melon head
mental
nana
pathetic
prune
silly billy
4 bumbreath
crazy
dap
derk
dick
dimwit

2 backward
banana head
bender
bighead
bird brain
bowl head
brat
burgerbrain
cabbage brain
cabbage head
clot
codger
Daphne
dappo
deacon
dimbrain
dingbat
dog

scum
Sidney
smiffy
spongecake
spud
zombie

5

SORT OF MEANINGLESS?

LOOK AT THE following passage from Michael Stubbs' book *Language, Schools and Classrooms*. This is taken from an actual interview, no matter how unreal it may look. (MS is Michael Stubbs and R and H are two girls from Edinburgh who have just listened to a tape recording of some children speaking dialect.)

R. Well, they sound sort of as if they weren't very well brought up theirselves, the way they were talking.

MS. Mmhm – what are you thinking of in particular?

H. Their grammar's pretty awful.

MS. What's pretty awful about it?

H. *It only sort of went in a little bit.* (Quoting from recording.)

MS. What's wrong with that?

H. Well, you don't sort of say that, do you?

MS. Well, what in particular?

H. It's bad English.

MS. Why?

H. Well, it just sounds bad English.

MS. Which bit of it then, or is it all . . .?

H. It only *sort of* went in.

MS. So, you don't say *sort of*?

H. I keep saying *sort of*, yeah, but you're not meant to say *sort of*.

MS. Well, I mean you said em *you don't sort of say that*, I think.

H. I know – you're not meant to say that sort of thing – and I know I shouldn't.

MS. Why not?

93

Sort of Meaningless?

H. It just doesn't sound right. It sounds as though you're Tarzan – Me Tarzan you Jane – Me speak English – sort of – I'm saying it again, aren't I?

MS. Well, don't you think it's quite a useful expression?

H. You get into the habit of using it, I won't say it again. I'll persevere and I won't say it. You get used to saying it if you hear other people saying it – you know you sort of – I'll never do it! – you associate that sort of thing with people who haven't really been taught to say it better.

The two girls hold opinions about language which may be rather similar to those of their parents and teachers. Of course, someone has taught them to dislike expressions like *sort of* and *y'know*. These expressions belong to the stigmatized elements of English grammar.

The quotation shows that not everyone speaks exactly in the way he or she wants to speak. In theory we may want our language to be free of small words like *y'know, now, sort of* and *well*. In theory we may also want our language to be free of swear-words, slang, neologisms and all that sort of thing. In practice, they are usually there.

Small words like these are especially tricky. They may pass unnoticed for a long period, but once they are discovered (or, rather, brought to our awareness) we hear them all the time. For example, there may be a new usage circulating in the language for a couple of years which is not discussed publicly, not even noticed. Speakers are not aware of it, but they use it and they hear it. Finally people become conscious of this strange creature in the language. They hear themselves use it and they certainly hear everyone else use it. Suddenly this seems to be the most common word in the English language. Probably it was just as common before. The difference is that we are aware of it now. The modern use of *hopefully* could be mentioned as an example of this type (see chapter 8).

As an example at a smaller level, suppose we are listening to someone. For ten minutes nothing remarkable happens. Suddenly we notice that this person says *y'know* all the time. It gets worse and worse, and soon we hear nothing but *y'know*. And, if this person isn't saying *y'know*, he's saying *well, all right* and *OK*. Besides, he isn't very interesting. Or, after half an hour in a lecture, someone's notes tail off into ⦀⦀. This shows that the 'listener' does not care about the content of the lecture or talk any more, but concentrates instead on one single formal aspect of the speaker's language. Whatever wisdom is presented goes unnoticed.

If anything is bad manners, this is. As listeners we should not behave like this. As speakers we should be aware that people might react in this way. The question is how to avoid this trap. We could try to be good speakers, whatever that means. But it is hardly possible to be aware of every single word or phrase that leaves our lips, especially the small ones. If we try to pay that much attention to our speech, it will probably be so slow and boring that no one will care to listen. We do not listen to speakers just because they happen to speak grammatical English – they must have something to say as well.

No, probably the only way around the problem is to be interesting and relevant. In addition, we should all try to follow the simple wisdom of this chapter: do not get upset because you find one or two words you do not like in the speech of your fellow human beings. Remember that you probably have one or two of them in your own speech.

WHY ALL THESE SMALL WORDS?

Why should so many people have such a strong disgust for what on the surface, at least, are rather innocent-looking creatures of language?

The main argument against expressions such as *y'know* and *sort of* is that they are unnecessary, that they are used simply as fillers – words that jump out of the mouth while we are figuring out what clever things to say next. We want to show, as linguists, that this argument is simply false.

Sort of Meaningless?

Look at this example.

OK, let's look at Turkey during the Middle Ages.

The OK here is not useless or redundant. It marks the end of whatever preceded this sentence and introduces the next subject matter. OK has a *textual function* here. An ordinary conversation, a speech, a lecture or any other act of speech consists of many utterances, of a long stretch of sounds with content. In writing, we separate the content not only into different sentences, but also into paragraphs, sections and chapters. In speech we do the same thing with the help of small words which show how different parts of the text are related to each other. OK can be used to introduce a new topic in the discourse.

Many other small words have other important conversational functions to do with change of topic and the point of what is being said. It is often hard for foreigners to learn how to use them correctly. Think of trying to teach a foreigner how to use *well, anyway, now then* or *oh* correctly.

Compare the following sentences.

(a) *I forgot the books.*
(b) *Oh, I forgot the books.*
(c) *Damn it, I forgot the books.*

Sentence (a) is a plain statement. Sentence (b) is not just (a) with some useless sound at the beginning. Rather, *oh* signals that the speaker has just remembered or realized something. Sentence (c) is much like (b). Swearing expressions do not add anything to the content of sentences. Instead, and in this they are like small words, they perform two functions. First, they signal something about what is happening in the mind of the speaker. In this way they are expressive. Second, they say something about how the listener should receive and/or react to the sentence.

Compare the *oh* sentence above with the *ah* sentence below.

Ah, this is the way to do it.

Here, *ah*, with the proper intonation, functions as an indication of something like 'I just realized'. In a cartoon it could be drawn with light bulb over the speaker's head.

People take turns as speakers and hearers. A turn may last from a second up to several minutes. It depends on the situation. When speakers start their turns, they often do this by acknowledging the preceding turn. This is typically done with *yes* or *yeah*, which does *not* mean that the speaker is answering a question or completely agreeing with the previous speaker. In this case, *yes* means that the speaker has understood what was said and taken it into consideration. After this the speaker is free to argue against what was just said. The *yes, but* sequence is common in English, as it is in other Germanic languages:

Yes, but I still do not think it is a good idea to have an alligator in the bathtub.

As speakers we want to know that the topics we introduce are of interest, that our views are not totally irrelevant, that what we say is understood and so on. Tag questions are typically used to ask for such confirmation:

Nice weather, isn't it?

Of course, speakers are capable of judging the quality of the weather all by themselves, but in this way they invite the listener to agree on this topic and discuss it further. In other situations, the speaker (a salesman or a politican, for example) can use this confirmation-seeking device to manipulate the hearer:

This Jaguar is the nicest car money can buy today, isn't it?
You can't really trust the Liberals, can you?

All the examples above show that these small words have a

role to play in language. They are always present in a conversation, in any ordinary spoken discourse. As we have shown, they have a number of different functions.

WHAT ARE THEY?

Quite a lot has been written about these small words in the field of linguistics, and people have come up with many terms for them. 'Small words' is certainly not a technical term. But what should they be called?

If we look in our traditional grammar books, we have two choices for a label. They could be *adverbs* and they could be *interjections*. In fact they are both adverb-like and interjection-like.

Adverbs are used to modify adjectives, verbs, other adverbs, and sentences. When these small words are used as adverbs, they modify the act of saying rather than what is said. When an utterance is opened up with *well*, this may tell the listener that the speaker does not entirely accept what has just been said:

> A. *It's wonderful, isn't it?*
> B. *Well, it's pretty good*

Ordinary adverbial phrases can have a double function. Sometimes they modify the sentence, sometimes the speech act. Compare these two sentences.

If the weather is nice tomorrow, we shall give a party at our house.
If you really want to know, we shall give a party at our house.

The first example shows the ordinary use of an adverbial phrase, in this case a conditional clause. What is said in the main clause is true if what is said in the *if* clause is true.

In the second example, the *if* clause modifies the act of saying the main clause – it functions as a *speech-act adverbial*. The *if* clause does not give a condition for the main clause to be true. The main clause is true whether or not the listener is interested in what the speaker has to say. When expressions like *oh, ah, OK, damn it* are used to modify a clause, they do so in a way similar to that described here.

Interjections are described in grammar books as having two main characteristics. They express something about the speaker's thoughts and emotions, and they have a rather free grammatical role. Many of these small words can be used as one-word utterances (*Oh!, Ah! Wow!, Damn!, OK,* etc.). Just how expressive they are depends on how much emphasis they are spoken with. *Ah!* can range from something rather indifferent to a *Wow!*

Sometimes these small words are called *evincives* when they function as interjections. Sometimes they are called *politeness* or *planning elements*, but it is hard to make these terms cover all the functions of small words. They are also often called *particles*, just to be on the safe side. Since particles don't change their form and can be different parts of speech, this term is neutral between the adverbial and the interjection properties of small words.

They have also been called *fillers, fumbles* and *hesitation sounds*. These terms do not give them much credit, and lead us to think of them as words or even noises produced while we are figuring out what to say. Their function would be something like 'Hold on, there is more to come. I just have to think of the right words to use.' Admittedly there are small words that work like this, the most common being *er-er*, but it is certainly not the most important or most typical function of these small words.

Er-er is socially rather interesting. It can be used to prevent others from coming into the discussion. Sometimes you can hear how the pitch of the *er-er* rises when the speaker notices that some other person is trying to take a turn.

Some people *er* more than others: males more than females, the middle class more than the working class. Since men with academic education *er* the most, they are also the hardest to interrupt, something we should not be proud of. At the turn of the century one Swedish professor of language noted this difference in the frequency of hesitation sounds between men and women and interpreted it as evidence for men's more careful thinking: women speak but men think first. This professor was not female. Besides, there is something strange about the principle that the more you *er*, the more you think.

Willis Edmondson and Juliane House have called these words *gambits* in their book *Let's Talk and Talk About It*. This term reflects how these words help to organize a spoken text into parts and sub-parts. Just to show that there are quite a few different types of small words (if we may still use that expression), we give the sub-classification of gambits presented by Edmondson and House.

UPTAKERS

RECEIPT

Meaning 'I've got you'
Phrases: *yes, yeah, hm, uh, I see, right, OK*
Example: *Yes, on the other hand, it's rather expensive.*

EXCLAIM

Meaning 'This is how I feel towards your message'
Phrases: *oh, ah really, oh dear, great, super, damn it*
Example: *Jesus Christ, I'm coming right away.*

GO ON

Meaning 'Go on speaking. I'm following'
Phrases: *Yes, yeah, hm, oh, good, fine, good heavens.*
Example: *Really!?!*

CLARIFIERS

CAJOLER

Meaning 'Please be agreeable to my message'

Phrases: *I mean, y'know, you see, honestly, actually, in fact*
Example: *Well, you see John, in fact, I'm rather busy at the moment.*

(Notice that *y'know* occurs in this list. This suggests that it is likely to be most heavily used by speakers who are not too sure of themselves or of how what they are saying will be received. We should perhaps therefore not be too surprised if younger people use it more often than older people.)

UNDERSCORER

Meaning 'Listen carefully now'
Phrases: *look, listen, the point is, just a minute, wait a sec*
Example: *Well, allright then, listen, we'll go down to the pub and talk to him tonight.*

APPEALER

Meaning 'Don't you think so too, hearer?'
Phrases: tag questions, *right, OK, (all) right, remember, eh*
Example: *Cost the earth, wouldn't it?*

STARTER

Meaning 'Hold on, I'm going to say something now'
Phrases: *well, now, OK*
Example: *Well, since last week I have been thinking about this communication problem.*

ASIDE

Meaning 'I'm talking to myself for a second'
Phrases: *let me see now, where was I?*
Example: *We train – what are they called in English? – mermaids.*

Sort of Meaningless?

When you speak a foreign language, you often say the asides in your native language. In whatever language they are given, they also are often accompanied by hand-waving and blurred pronunciation. The point isn't to give information but to make the listener understand that you are thinking.

A conversation without any of these small words would sound peculiar and unnatural. The best proof that we need these phrases probably comes from a simple test that everyone can do while speaking on the phone. When you are listening to a person who has a lot to say, listen to yourself also. You will hear yourself saying *hmm, oh dear, yeah,* etc., at intervals of a second or two. Try to keep quiet. After five or ten seconds, you will hear a worried voice saying, 'Hello, are you still there?'

This shows how common and indispensable these small words are when the feedback must be given vocally. In face-to-face conversations, we often nod or glance at someone instead of giving a vocal feedback. In fact, if you send out vocal feedback in ordinary conversations as often as you do in telephone conversations, it sounds very strange. The speaker will probably be irritated with you and think that you are not very relaxed. Try it.

We have written quite a few words in defence of these small words in this chapter. However, we do not claim that each and every small word ever uttered was right to the point, well planned and purposeful. Sometimes people come out with things like the following, which we have not made up. We will not argue that these sentences are something to be proud of.

I mean, I mean she's so little, I mean you, you know sort of one can imagine a sort of middle-aged woman with a coat that seemed you know sort of just slightly exaggerated her form. You know, I mean she could sort of slip things inside pockets.

A LITTLE BIT OF THEORY

Here is a very simple picture of a speech act. There is a speaker, a listener and a world around them. Between them there is an utterance, here called a *text*.

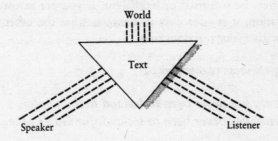

The text has three functions or gives out three types of information. Following the German linguist and psychologist Karl Bühler, we may characterize them in the following way.

Symbol function   This is what we usually call meaning. Words are symbols: e.g. the word *horse* refers to four-legged mammals which you can ride and bet on. This function is always present in acts of speaking, we hope. There are no conversations about nothing at all. (However, some come rather close.)

Symptom function   This reveals what kind of person the speaker is. Just imagine yourself picking up the telephone and hearing a voice you never heard before. After a few seconds you usually can tell whether the person speaking is a man or a woman, young or old, a native or a foreigner. You may guess something about the speaker's geographical and social background. You may also pick up some clues about the person's state of mind – whether he or she is glad or sad, relaxed or nervous. We cannot open our mouths without sending out this type of information.

Sort of Meaningless?

Signal function   Every utterance is directed towards someone. It has a purpose and it should be reacted to. Questions ask the listener for information and orders tell the listener to do something. Even plain statements need some kind of reaction. If someone just walks in the room and says 'Margaret Thatcher is the nicest woman I have ever seen', you should react in some way or other – agree or disagree, be surprised or indifferent. If you are involved in a conversation, it is your duty to consider what the other person says and give your reactions to it.

Compare these two sentences:

> *Henry has never been to Iceland in the winter.*
> *Henry has never been to Iceland, for God's sake.*

The sentences are identical up to the phrase at the end. These two phrases are very different from each other. Whereas *in the winter* relates directly to the content of the sentence, it is hard to see how *for God's sake* does, since it does not have much of a symbol function. But it does have both a symptom and a signal function. With the proper intonation this phrase may be a symptom of an irritated speaker, and then it will be a signal to the preceding speaker to remember this fact about Henry's travels once and for all.

The typical function of the small words we have discussed in this chapter is to function as symptoms and signals. Their contribution as symbols in language is rather poor. This is one reason for their low status in studies of language, where there is a great concentration on the symbolic function. The phrase *sort of* has little symbolic function, which is why people often say that it is 'meaningless', but it *does* signal uncertainty about whether one is expressing oneself accurately or not.

Another reason for the low status of small words is their close ties with the spoken language. We are so used to studying the written language at school that we actually believe that the spoken language either is, or at least should be, like the written language.

However, it never is. And it shouldn't be. In a conversation, we often talk about what we have in front of us. We can use expressions like *here, there, on the top, further back, closer, stop! good!* and they will be specific enough. The spoken language is typically a language of *here* and *now*, while the written language is typically a language of *there* and *then*.

THE WORLDS OF CONVERSATION

Spoken language is often described by different sports metaphors – chess and tennis are commonly used. In the context of small words, poker is probably better. All these small words show that we are bad poker-players. We do not keep a good poker face when we play our words, when we take our turns. By using these small words, we react to what others say, indicate our feelings about what we say ourselves, and point to how the listener should understand our utterances.

When we talk, we enter into a conversation from our own *private world* of knowledge and beliefs. The speaker has one such world and the listener another. During the conversation, we together build up a shared world of discourse. The small words we have been talking about rise like bubbles out of our private worlds up to the surface of the *shared world*. They help to give indications to do with surprise, irritation, insecurity, and so on, about the relationship between the private world and the shared worlds without forcing us to spell out the whole story word for word. This description of the worlds of conversation is based on the terminology of the American linguist Lawrence Schourup.

These small words are not meaningless or useless in language. They are meaningful – without carrying a heavy load of meaning. They are very functional. It is hard even to imagine a human language without them, isn't it?

6

RIGHT OR WRONG?

ALOT OF NATIVE speakers of the English language worry from time to time about whether what they say is *correct English* or not. In certain social situations, very many of us are scared stiff about 'making mistakes' in our English. Some people are so worried about this that they actually answer advertisements in newspapers from companies that make money by playing on these fears. 'Have you ever been let down by your English?' they ask. 'Have you ever been ashamed of the way you speak?' If you have, they hope you will write away to them, and they will send you booklets about how to put this shameful problem right.

We think this attitude, which is extremely widespread, is deplorable. In our view it is very sad that millions of people are inhibited about expressing themselves by the sincere but erroneous belief that they cannot speak their own language properly. There is absolutely no need for them to feel this way. People who have learnt the English language as their first language in infancy and have spoken it all their lives make very few mistakes in their everyday speech.

MISTAKES IN YOUR OWN LANGUAGE?

Speaking your own language is not like speaking a foreign language that you have studied in school or that you have tried to learn as an adult. All of us make mistakes when we are beginning to learn a foreign language. Only a very small number of adults manage to learn a foreign language so well that no one can tell that it is not their native language. Most people make mistakes and get things wrong in foreign languages. English-speakers are very familiar with foreigners saying things like *I am knowing it very well*, *He didn't came* and *Why you did this?* These things are *mistakes*, and no native speaker would ever say them, except as a joke. If you were teaching a foreigner to speak English, or if you heard a three-year-old child saying these things, you would probably find some way of indicating that they were *wrong*, and that there is a *correct* way of saying them, namely *I know it very well*, *He didn't come* and *Why did you do that?*

But native speakers do not make mistakes of this sort because they have learnt their language from infancy at a time in their lives when humans are programmed to learn languages. Native speakers master the rules of the language perfectly, without being conscious of what those rules are. For instance, although they are not aware of this fact, native speakers of English know the rules that govern the order of words and the use of the auxiliary verb *do* in English questions and negative sentences. See if you can work out what the rule is from the following sentences, some of which are grammatical and some not (those marked*). Keep in mind (if English is your native language) that your brain already worked it out for you long ago when you were a very small child, without anybody actually telling you what the rule was.

They want to swim.
They don't want to swim.
**They wantn't to swim.*

They can swim.
**They don't can swim.*
They can't swim.

Do they want to swim?
**Want they to swim?*
Don't they want to swim?
**Wantn't they to swim?*

**Do they can swim?*
Can they swim?
**Don't they can swim?*
Can't they swim?

They do want to swim.
They want to swim and so do I.

**They do can swim.*
**They can swim and so do I.*

*They want to swim and so want I.

They can swim and so can I.

No native speaker would use constructions like those marked*. Those are genuine mistakes in English usage.

We believe, as do most linguists, that native speakers do not make mistakes. Native speakers for the most part speak their native language perfectly. Of course, there are errors which all of us can make from time to time. We can all, for example, make slips of the tongue, and say things we didn't intend to say, like *How many of there are them?* rather than *How many of them are there?* And we can all get in a muddle with long sentences and change the construction halfway through, as in *There's a man over there who I don't know who he is*; or *I wonder who those people who I always see him over the park on Thursdays with*. And we can all use words without knowing what they really mean – as we shall see in our discussion of malapropisms in chapter 8. But with these exceptions, we feel happy about claiming that native speakers always speak correct English.

If we, as linguists, feel this way about it, the question then arises, where do attitudes about correctness come from? We want to argue that those people who say that some things in English are right and other things are wrong are themselves wrong. But where do their – very widespread – views originate? Why do people believe that it is *wrong* to say *I done it*, or *It was me that did it*, or *I'm different to what he is*?

There are a number of different explanations we can give for this very common phenomenon. One obvious point is that there is a strong tendency for people to dislike innovations and regard them as being mistakes or incorrect. In spite of the fact that nearly everybody now says *Hopefully it won't rain*, there are still people around, and probably will be for some time yet, who think that it's wrong. (See chapter 8 for more on this.)

LATIN

As we saw in chapter 1, another factor we have to consider when we are thinking about the origins of notions of correctness is the influence of Latin. In the twentieth century there is a convention in the English-speaking world that books, newspapers, journals, and so on, should be written in Standard English, and not in any other dialect of the language. We have kept to this convention in this book. If we had written the previous sentence as *Another factor we has to consider when we be a-thinking about the origins of notions of correctness be the influence of Latin*, the publisher would probably not have liked it, and everybody else would have found it very strange and probably comic. Breaking social conventions leads to this sort of reaction.

One interesting thing about social conventions, though, is that they change. Anyone writing a serious academic work 500 years ago in *any* form of English would have had the same type of reaction. In mediaeval times the social convention was that Latin was the only language in which theological, philosophical and academic works could be written. People attempting to write such works in English, French or Dutch would have been subject to ridicule. Latin was considered to be good, correct, appropriate, flexible, expressive, and so on, just as Standard English is today, and the vernacular languages were considered to be inferior. Latin was an international language of learning in Europe, and it was associated with the Church and the Bible. It also had the advantage of being a dead language with no native speakers and therefore not subject to change.

WHICH SHORES DO PREPOSITIONS GET STRANDED ON?

This led to a view which survived even into more modern times (when English *was* being used for serious purposes) that, because Latin was a superior language to English (which of course it actually wasn't), then, at those points where the two languages differed, Latin must be right and English wrong. A number of people therefore tried to change the structure of English at some points to make it resemble Latin more closely. For instance, it has always been normal in English and related languages such as Swedish to end sentences with a preposition. You could say things like *I have a new house which I'm very pleased with*. It was argued, however, that this grammatical structure was 'wrong' and that one ought to say *I have a new house with which I'm very pleased*, because in Latin it was not grammatical to end sentences with a preposition, any more than it is in modern languages descended from Latin, such as French. Thus in Swedish you can say

Jag har ett nytt hus   som jag är väldigt nöjd med
I have a new house which I am very pleased with

whereas in French you certainly cannot say

J'ai une nouvelle maison que je suis très content de.

However, in spite of the naturalness and long history of this construction in the Germanic languages, the argument was that, if it was wrong in Latin, it was wrong in English. It is still possible to find books on English usage that will tell you that it is 'incorrect' to end sentences with prepositions. In fact, most people over the age of forty have probably been told by schoolteachers that they should not do so. As a consequence, although the attempt to rid English of a natural usage has not been successful, this construction is still avoided by many writers, especially in more formal styles. It is thus still more formal style to write *I have a new house with which I am very pleased* than *I have a new house which I am very pleased with*.

IT'S ONLY US

Other features are often considered to be errors because of this continuing inferiority complex of English with respect to Latin. A good example is the use of what linguists call the oblique pronouns in English, such as *me*, *him*, and *us*. One usage of these pronouns is in sentences like *It's me!*, *It was him that did it*, *This is her*. This is a very old construction in English, and it is also found in other languages, this time including French : *C'est moi!* (It's me). However, such constructions were not found in Latin. The grammatical structure of Latin required that only nouns and pronouns in the nominative case could occur together with *esse*, the verb 'to be'. This led to the argument that in English, too, we should use nominative pronouns and say *It's I!*, *It was he that did it*, *This is she*.

These sentences sound very strange to most English speakers. And the equivalents in French are even more ludicrous: *C'est je!* is just totally impossible in French as a way of saying 'It's me'. The reason for this is that neither English nor French really has the grammatical distinction between nominative and accusative case that was present in Latin. If a noun in Latin was the subject of the verb it was in the nominative case and had one set of endings. If it was the object of a verb (or of certain prepositions) it was in the accusative case and had another set of endings. Thus

> *Rex puellam amat*, 'The king loves the girl'

but

> *Regem puella amat*, 'The girl loves the king'

English and French do not have case endings of this type. The only forms in English which behave in a way which is at all similar to Latin are the personal pronouns. Most English pronouns have two different forms depending on grammatical context: *I*, *me*; *he*, *him*;

she, her; we, us; they, them. However, it is not legitimate to refer to these as 'nominative' and 'accusative' forms as if they were Latin. It is true that the forms *I, he, she, we, they* do occur only as the subject of verbs, like the Latin nominative. But it is *not* true that the forms *me, him, her, us, them* occur only as objects.

A better description of what happens in natural native-speaker English is that *I, he, she, we, they* occur as the subjects of verbs where the pronoun in question is the only subject that the verb has. In all other cases, such as where the pronoun occurs as an object, where the pronoun stands on its own, where the pronoun occurs in apposition after the verb *be*, or where there is more than one subject, then the oblique case pronouns *me, him, her, us, them* are found. Thus, if someone asks *Who won?* we could answer *They did*, using *they* because here it is the subject of the verb *did*. But we could also answer the question *Who won?* without using a verb, in which case we would have to reply *Them*. English speakers do not say *Who won? They.* Only *Who won? Them*, and *Who won? They did* occur.

We illustrate these points in the following table. Note that only in one set of forms – set 5, where they are single subjects – are the 'nominative' pronouns genuinely natural in most dialects of English. (There are, however, rural dialects in the South of England and in Newfoundland where it is natural to say *I gave it to he* and *John saw we not they*. And there are also dialects in the South-west of England where it is possible to say *Us cried*. But these are different issues.)

NATURAL ENGLISH	UNNATURAL ENGLISH
1 *Jane saw me*	*Jane saw I*
Jane saw him	*Jane saw he*
Jane saw her	*Jane saw she*
Jane saw us	*Jane saw we*
Jane saw them	*Jane saw they*
2 *Jane gave it to me*	*Jane gave it to I*

Jane gave it to him	*Jane gave it to he*
Jane gave it to her	*Jane gave it to she*
Jane gave it to us	*Jane gave it to we*
Jane gave it to them	*Jane gave it to they*

3
If you were me	*If you were I*
That'll be him	*That'll be he*
It was her	*It was she*
It was us	*It was we*
It is them	*It is they*

4
Who won? Me	*Who won? I*
Who lost? Him	*Who lost? He*
Who shouted? Her	*Who shouted? She*
Who cried? Us	*Who cried? We*
Who arrived? Them	*Who arrived? They*

5
I won	*Me won*
He lost	*Him lost*
She shouted	*Her shouted*
We cried	*Us cried*
They arrived	*Them arrived*

There is a particularly interesting phenomenon in English, however, when there is more than one subject of a verb and at least one of them is a pronoun. For a long time there has been considerable freedom of usage and variation between dialects and between speakers as to what happens in sentences of this type. Which of the following versions do you prefer?

> *Me and him are going to the party.*
> *Him and me are going to the party.*
> *I and he are going to the party.*
> *He and I are going to the party.*

The *I and he* version is particularly unnatural, but all the others certainly occur in modern English. And how do you feel about these sentences?

> *Us and her are going to the party.*
> *Her and us are going to the party.*
> *We and she are going to the party.*
> *She and we are going to the party.*

As we have seen, some people who have been seduced by the prestige of Latin have argued that some of the unnatural English forms are 'correct' and that the natural English forms are 'wrong'. They sometimes argue that we *ought* to say *Who's there? I!* or *Who won? They!* These arguments have had very little success, although we must confess that there are some Americans who have been bullied into answering the telephone as follows:

> – *May I speak to Mary, please?*
> – *This is she.*

Because of the variety of forms and the freedom already present in English, however, the pedants have been much more successful in arguing that it is also wrong to say things like *Him and me are going to the party, John and me did it, Her and us are going to the party, Her and John are coming*, and so on, because after all Latin did not use sentences of this form. These arguments about two or more subject pronouns in a sentence have not by any means been successful in removing the use of the pronouns *me, him, her, us, them* from the language in such expressions in favour of *I, he, she, we, they*. But they have created considerable insecurity in the minds of many speakers about the 'correctness' of their language and considerable misunderstanding of schoolteachers' exhortations. This in turn has led to the development of some new forms.

HYPERCORRECTIONS

For instance, because we have been told that it is 'incorrect' or 'bad English' to say *John and me did it* and that we should change this to *John and I did it*, many people have become very uncomfortable about expressions such as *John and me* altogether. They therefore start changing *John and me* to *John and I* everywhere, and not just where the Latin-influenced pedants think they ought to. We thus encounter people saying not only *John and I did it* but also *Jane gave it to John and I*. This of course was originally a totally unnatural English construction. We would certainly still tell foreigners learning English that it is a mistake, but, if it continues to grow in popularity, it may well one day actually become natural English. But it will have become natural because of speakers trying to change the way they speak to fit in with some unnatural model. Because the model is unnatural, they get it wrong, extend the change into inappropriate grammatical contexts, and produce forms which no one ever intended that they should use and that have nothing to do with Latin!

It is in fact quite possible that pronoun hypercorrection will become the norm eventually. It is now particularly common to hear speakers say things such as *between you and I*, where of course the rules of both Latin and English grammar require *between you and me*, and *He told John and I about it*, although of course they would never say *He told I about it*. We have not yet heard anybody say *I told John and they about it*, but it is probably only a matter of time. We have certainly seen in newspapers as distinguished as the British *Observer* sentences such as *There was an excellent rapport between he and his mother*. This is a classic case of linguistic *hypercorrection*: we 'correct' ourselves not only when we should but also when we should not. This is a perfect way of making a fool of yourself.

SOCIALIZING WITH GRAMMAR

However, perhaps the most powerful source of judgements about correctness in English has to do with the relationship between language and social class. The fact is that many forms which are considered to be 'bad English' are simply forms which are typical of lower-class dialects. On the other hand, forms which are considered to be 'correct' are very often associated with the speech of the upper class and upper middle class, who speak a dialect which is known as Standard English. This is also the dialect normally used in writing English and which we usually teach to foreigners.

It is widely agreed by many people who believe themselves to be experts on the English language, but who are really not, that it is incorrect to say *I done it*. This is actually a rather strange thing for anyone to believe because it is quite clear that this form is used by a majority of native English-speakers around the world. The so-called 'correct' form *I did it* is normally used by only a minority of native speakers – certainly no more than 30 per cent. Why is it then that the majority are said to be wrong while the minority are said to be right? This has to do with who uses which form. As will be obvious to anyone who has grown up in the British Isles, North America or Australasia, the minority of people who say *I did it* are those who on average have more wealth, power, status and education than those who say *I done it* (of course, we can make no claims about every single individual). It is therefore not surprising that *I done it* has less prestige, and that this lower prestige leads this verb form to be regarded as undesirable and therefore wrong. It is of course not 'wrong' in any meaningful sense of the word to say *I done it*, but it is an indication of relatively low social status. We cannot say that a form that most people use is a 'mistake'. We can say, however, that it is typical of lower-class dialects. Because of the way in which our society is structured, it is a form which can on occasions put its users at a social disadvantage.

Right or Wrong?

RATIONALIZING PREJUDICE

Most native English speakers today live in societies which subscribe to an egalitarian and democratic philosophy. It is not appropriate in these societies to be seen to discriminate against people on the grounds of their social background. Teachers therefore cannot say to children 'Don't say *I done it* – it betrays your low social status.' Instead, rationalizations have to be developed for why such forms are to be avoided. One such rationalization is, as we have seen, that *I done it* and other such forms are wrong. People in education have sometimes tended to regard *I done it* as being on a par with $2 \times 2 = 5$. It should be obvious however that $2 \times 2 = 4$ is inherently true, and that, if it were not, the world, and indeed the universe, would be a very different place. There is nothing, on the other hand, that is inherently true about *I did it*. It would not make any difference to anything important if every native speaker of English went around saying *I done it*. In fact, a majority of them already do.

Another rationalization is that *I done it* is confusing because *done* is 'really' the past participle of *do*, as in *I have done it*, and that to use it 'instead of' *did* is to lose the distinction. This is of course a ludicrous argument, because no native speaker is likely to confuse *I have done it* with *I done it*. In any case, the vast majority of verbs in English show no difference between the past participle and the past tense anyway: for instance, *I have played it* versus *I played it*.

Yet another rationalization is that *I done it* is 'bad grammar' or 'ungrammatical'. This requires some discussion. Linguists know that all languages have grammar – it is an essential characteristic of human languages. However, the grammar of different languages differs, sometimes very dramatically. Even quite closely related languages have different grammatical rules. For example, German requires the verb to be the second grammatical element in any main clause. English does not have such a rule, and we therefore do not say *Today went I to the cinema* (as would be required in German).

Equally, all dialects have grammatical rules. It is, once again, simply the case that structures differ somewhat from dialect to dialect. Unlike non-native speakers, native speakers do not make grammatical errors. They do, however, use grammatical rules which differ from those of Standard English but which are still grammatical for all that. We can illustrate this as follows.

English has two different verbs *to do*. One is a main verb which is used to talk about somebody actually doing something, as in *I always do my work*. The other is an auxiliary verb without any real meaning which is used in negation, as in *I don't like it*, and in questions, as in *Do you want some?* The grammatical structure of the English dialect we call Standard English has a distinction between the past tense form *did* and the past participle form *done*. Most nonstandard dialects do not have this distinction, using *done* in both cases. On the other hand, most nonstandard dialects make a distinction which Standard English does not make between the main verb past tense *done* and auxiliary past tense *did*. It would be ungrammatical in the nonstandard dialects to say *You done it, done you?*, which is why of course nobody ever says it.

STANDARD ENGLISH

| Main verb | *You do it,* | *You did it,* | *You've done it* |
| Auxiliary | *do you?* | *did you?* | |

NONSTANDARD DIALECTS

| Main verb | *You do it,* | *You done it,* | *You've done it* |
| Auxiliary | *do you?* | *did you?* | |

It would be foolish to claim that the nonstandard dialects are superior to the standard dialect because they make this distinction between auxiliary and main verbs. But it is equally absurd to claim that Standard English is superior to the other dialects because it makes a distinction between the past tense and past participle. The fact is quite simply that different dialects do things differently, just as different languages do. No sensible German-speaker would ever say, we hope, that English is ungrammatical because its speakers say *Today I went to the cinema*. And no sensible Standard English-speaker should say that nonstandard dialects are ungrammatical because they allow forms like *I done it*. It is ungrammatical to say *I done it* in *Standard* English, but it is *not* ungrammatical to say *I done it* in *English*.

Forms such as *I done it*, and other lower-class dialect forms such as *a man what I know*, *he ain't got it*, *we don't want none*, *them books over there*, *he hurt hisself*, *she writ a letter*, and so on, are not ungrammatical. No one should be ashamed of using them or believe that they are making a mistake if they do. Of course, in many educational, social and occupational contexts, people may be discriminated against for employing grammatical forms typical of lower-status social-class dialects. If they want to avoid this discrimination, they can try to avoid using these forms. But they should be clear about why they are doing this – they are doing it for social and not for linguistic reasons.

TO TALK GRAMMAR

HIGGINS. (to Pickering reflectively) *You see the diffi-culty?*

PICKERING. *Eh? What difficulty?*

HIGGINS. *To get her to talk grammar. The mere pronunciation is easy enough.*

LIZA. *I don't want to talk grammar. I want to talk like a lady in a flower-shop*

Bernard Shaw, *Pygmalion*

GRAMMAR AND SUCCESS

Prejudice against lower-class dialects is not dissimilar to racial and sexual prejudice. We believe that it is highly undesirable and that it is our job as linguists to work against ignorance about dialect differences and for greater dialect tolerance. Unlike racial and sexual prejudice, however, it is possible to guard oneself against dialect prejudice by changing one's dialect, or by mastering an additional dialect, if one wishes. In an ideal and truly egalitarian and democratic society, it would not be necessary to do this. In our society, however, many people are under considerable pressure to do so. Teachers are therefore entirely justified in teaching pupils who do not use Standard English how to write this dialect so that they can protect themselves against this prejudice and advance socially, educationally, occupationally and economically if they wish. We do not want children to leave school only to suffer as cannon fodder in the job market.

We should all be aware, however, that changing your dialect is not necessarily an easy thing to do successfully. Also, there may be psychological costs in terms of personal and social identity. Most people, as our statistics show, do prefer to continue speaking their native nonstandard dialects (if they didn't, Standard English would now be the majority dialect, of course). They should not be made to feel that there is anything wrong about this. Their English may not be socially as 'good' as that of certain other speakers, but expressively and in every other way it certainly is.

7

Bad Accents?

As we saw in the first chapter of this book, everybody has an accent. Your accent is simply the way you pronounce, and, since you can't speak without pronouncing, you have an accent just as much as anybody else. An interesting problem for linguists, though, is where all these different accents come from. Why is it that Americans sound different from English people? Why don't speakers in the south of England pronounce English in the same way as speakers from the north? Why do people in Wolverhampton have somewhat different accents from people in Birmingham?

The answer to all these questions has to do with change in language. We do not altogether understand why languages change, but it is a fact that they do. Speakers in different parts of the English-speaking world pronounce English in different ways because of changes that have and have not taken place in their area. For example, 600 years ago, all English-speakers used to say 'oot' and 'hoose' for *out* and *house*. Now only speakers in Scotland and certain areas of the north of England say this, because everywhere else the pronunciation has changed to 'owt' and 'howse'. Similarly, people in the north of England still say 'oop' and 'coop', as all English-speakers used to until about 400 years ago, rather than the newer forms *up*, and *cup*, which speakers elsewhere use.

A LUVVLY ACCENT WITH A CLEAH SOUND

New pronunciations start life in a particular location and then spread from there to neighbouring areas. They only rarely affect the whole of the language area, and this gives rise to regionally different accents. Think about these different pronunciations of the phrase *A lovely hill with a clear view*:

SCOTLAND	A luvvly hill with a clearr view
LANCASHIRE	A loovly ill with a clearr view
YORKSHIRE	A loovly ill with a cleah view
NORFOLK	A luvvly hill with a cleah voo
LONDON	A luvvly ill with a cleah view
BRISTOL	A luvvly ill with a clearr view
BBC	A luvvly hill with a cleah view

The differences between these accents as far as this phrase is concerned are due to the different distribution of old and new forms. Each of the accents, including the statusful BBC accent, has accepted some of the innovations and not others:

	NEW FORM	OLD FORM
lovely	luvvly	loovly
hill	ill	hill
clear	cleah	clearr
view	voo	view

It would be a mistake, however, to assume that all differences in pronunciation are regional. Just as different changes take place in different areas and give rise to different regional accents, so different changes also occur among different social groups, and then spread from them to other – but unusually not all – social groups. This naturally gives rise to different social accents.

REGIONAL AND SOCIAL ACCENTS

If we consider how our phrase *A lovely hill with a clear view* is pronounced in London, it is obvious that the London pronunciation given above is something of a simplification. A more accurate representation would take account of social class:

UPPER MIDDLE	A luvvly hill with a cleah view
LOWER MIDDLE	A luvvly hioo with a cleah view
UPPER WORKING	A luvvly ioo with a cleah view
LOWER WORKING	A luvvly ioo wiv a cleah view

In Britain, accent differences are both regional and social, but it is the social differences that, for the most part, produce judgements about good and bad accents. A great many British people consider it to be a Good Thing to pronounce the *h* in *hill*, *house* and *hammer*, and a Bad Thing to say 'ill', 'ouse' and 'ammer'.

The reason for this sentiment is obviously the same as the one we advanced in connection with judgements about grammar in chapter 6. In middle-class accents, including especially the BBC accent, *h* is pronounced in words such as these, whereas in many lower-class regional accents it is not. Judgements about 'correct pronunciation' are really social judgements about the status in our society of particular social accents. Of course, once again the complainers have thought up a number of rationalizations for why it is 'wrong' to say 'ammer', so as not to appear to be discriminating against speakers from lower social groups. They will say that not pronouncing *h* is slovenly, careless, lazy and wrong, and that the *h* ought to be pronounced because it is there in the spelling.

The reason why *h* is pronounced in some accents and not others actually has to do with change rather than with 'slovenliness'. In some parts of the country, such as Scotland and Northumberland, and in some social accents, such as the BBC accent, *h* has never been lost, whereas in most other accents it has been. Those who pronounce *h* have therefore retained an older pronunciation. People from Newcastle are not actually more careful than people from Lancashire. In this particular case, they just retain in their accents a more conservative pronunciation.

We have to say, moreover, that 'older' does not in any way mean 'better'. Change in language no more means disease and decay in pronunciation than it does in grammar or vocabulary. If the only correct pronunciation was the older pronunciation, then the only correct way to pronounce the phrase we used above would

---

Social-class dialect

As children, we lived on the lower-class fringe of an upper-class suburb.... In the next street, by the railway, lived the rough children. Shrill, grubby, with torn clothes, they suffered one handicap in particular which, in my parents' eyes, made them unsuitable for me to play with. Their speech was horribly uncouth. In the street on the other side, by the park, lived the posh children. They had pleasanter ways and were nicely dressed; best of all, they spoke with mild and expensive voices. But with these, too, I had nothing to do. We could not, without embarrassment, ask them home to tea in our small house.

So, at an early age, I ran into the phenomenon of class, and the speech differences bound up with it; and fenced in by solemn snobberies I learnt to walk the narrow way between two worlds, having, I suspected, less fun than either.

S. J. Sharpless, quoted in R. Quirk, The Use of English

---

be 'A loovly hill with a clearr view'. This is a pronunciation you might be able to find in small areas of the north-east of England, but it is not used anywhere else, and certainly not by BBC newsreaders. It is not 'careless' to omit the *h* in *hill* any more than it is to omit the *r* in *clear*, as the BBC accent does. The fact that Scottish and West-of-England accents pronounce the *r* in *clear* does not make them superior to the BBC accent. And people from Lancashire are not more careful than people from Newcastle because they, too, keep the older pronunciation with the *r*.

Compare the historical loss of *h* and *r* with the loss of *k*. No one would want to claim that it is 'lazy' to 'drop' the *k* in *knee* and *know*. You have to drop the *k* in modern English – you would be thought very funny if you didn't – although until about 400 years ago it was pronounced by all speakers. And, if *k*-dropping is not 'lazy', then *h*-dropping cannot be lazy either.

The fact is that modern English spelling is a rather good indication of medieval English pronunciation but a very bad guide to how English should be pronounced today. This is because most of the changes which have taken place in English pronunciation in the past few centuries have not been matched by corresponding changes in spelling. Spelling can therefore not be used as evidence for how a word ought to be pronounced in modern English.

It is a fact that the *h* used to be pronounced in English not only in words such as *hill* and *house* but also in words such as *night, eight, weigh* – that's why these words have an *h* in their spelling. Nobody would now seriously suggest, we hope, that we ought to return to this pronunciation. And there are some words in English where the *h* has *never* been pronounced, such as *hour* and *honest*; again, we assume that nobody would want this *h* to be pronounced. No, the only reason why we find so much prejudice against *h*-dropping in modern English is that it is associated with lower-social-class accents. If anyone doubts where this association comes from, look at these figures about h-dropping taken from urban dialect surveys.

H-dropping by speakers of different social classes in Norwich and Bradford (percentages)

	NORWICH	BRADFORD
Upper middle class	6	12
Lower middle class	14	28
Upper working class	40	67
Middle working class	60	89
Lower working class	60	93

The relationship between pronunciation and social background is unmistakable. Different social accents have different pronunciations, just as different regional accents do. Social accents are not bad in any linguistic sense. Nor are any individual vowel or consonant pronunciations bad in themselves. It must be clear that, if it is not bad to pronounce *hour* and *our* identically, it cannot be bad to pronounce *hill* and *ill* the same either.

The only bad thing about lower-social-class accents is that they symbolize low social status. The majority of people who do not speak with a BBC accent therefore run the risk of being discriminated against by undemocratic individuals and institutions in certain social and occupational situations. This discrimination is naturally something which some people will want to guard themselves against by acquiring the ability to speak with a higher-status accent. Others may not want to suffer from the insecurities which often accompany speaking in a variety other than the one which they have grown up with, and will prefer to continue to remain true to their regional and social roots. Some will try to have it both ways, using higher-status forms in formal and professional situations and their original speech in informal situations with family and friends. A few may want to fight openly against the irrational prejudices which a majority of English accents suffer from by pointing to accent discrimination as an anti-democratic phenomenon not totally unlike racial prejudice and sexual discrimination. We would consider any of these reactions to be entirely rational and sensible.

UGLY ACCENTS

The other general argument that we often hear about 'bad pronunciation' has to do with the perception that some accents are 'ugly'. People who are otherwise very prepared to acknowledge that no one accent or dialect is superior to any other are sometimes all the same prepared to argue that some varieties of language are actually more aesthetically pleasing than others. We do not believe that this is true, or, at least, we believe that it is true only in a very complicated sort of way. It is possible to show, in fact, that people's apparently aesthetic evaluations of accents are just as much social evaluations as are their judgements about correctness. If we find some accents ugly and other accents pleasing, this has to do with the *social connotations* that these accents have for us.

This will be true, we believe, for any variety of any language. We are prepared to bet, for example, that no reader of this book will have different aesthetic responses to the various dialects of Vietnamese unless they are familar with the language and with the culture which it comes from. For most Westerners, different varieties of Vietnamese have no social connotations that differentiate one from the other, and we therefore do not respond with differentiated aesthetic evaluations.

THE NOTE TAKER. *A woman who utters such depressing and disgusting sounds has no right to be anywhere – no right to live. Remember that you are a human being with a soul and the divine gift of articulate speech: that your native language is the language of Shakespear and Milton and The Bible; and dont sit there crooning like a bilious pigeon.*

THE FLOWER GIRL (quite overwhelmed, looking up at him in mingled wonder and deprecation without daring to raise her head). *Ah-ah-ah-ow-ow-ow-oo!*

THE NOTE TAKER (whipping out his book). *Heavens! what a sound!* (He writes: then holds out the book and reads, reproducing her vowels exactly). *Ah-ah-ah-ow-ow-ow-oo!*

Bernard Shaw, *Pygmalion*

AN EXPERIMENT

In the 1970s an experiment was carried out on 'ugly' and 'beautiful' English accents that showed how very much our 'aesthetic' responses are socially conditioned (H. Giles and P. Trudgill, 'Sociolinguistics and linguistic value judgements', in P. Trudgill, *On Dialect*). It went like this. A tape-recording was made of ten different people with ten different British English accents reading the same short passage. This recording was then played to different groups of English listeners, who were asked to rate the speakers on a number of counts, including how pleasant or unpleasant they sounded. The listeners were also asked to say where they thought the speakers came from, and nearly all the listeners recognized nearly all the accents. There was also a high level of agreement among these listeners' evaluations. The rank order of the ten different accents on the pleasant–unpleasant dimension was

1   BBC accent
2   Welsh accent
3   Yorkshire accent
4   Irish accent
5   Geordie accent
6   West Country accent
7   Glasgow accent
8   Liverpool accent
9   Birmingham accent
10 London (Cockney) accent

Now, you could say that, if large numbers of English people all agree to a considerable extent about what is nice and what is nasty, then they can't all be wrong. But there is a sense in which they are. The first thing you can notice about this list is the way in which the accents at the bottom of the list are all from large urban areas. Then come the more rural accents. And then at the top of the list is the BBC accent. We argue on the basis of this list that the preference for rural over urban accents has to do with the associations people have with these varieties. Urban accents are disliked beause they have connotations – for the overwhelmingly urban British population – of smoke, grime, heavy industry and work, while rural accents are associated with clean air and holidays. The BBC accent is considered the nicest, we suggest, because it is associated with education, wealth, power, status and prestige.

ACROSS THE ATLANTIC

This was confirmed by the second stage of the experiment. For this it was necessary to find groups of listeners who could understand the tape-recording but who would not be aware of what the connotations of the different accents were. For this reason, the recording was played to a number of groups of native English-speakers in Canada and the United States. These North Americans did not know what the accents on the recordings were or where the speakers were from. Indeed, they failed in some cases to recognize the accents as those of native speakers – the Scot was in some cases labelled as Mexican, for instance, and the Welsh speaker as coming from Norway!

Because they did not know where the speakers came from, they could not and did not have any connotations associated with the accents. There were two exceptions – they did recognize the BBC accent and the London accent. We would therefore expect the North American listeners, when asked to evalute the accents as pleasant or unpleasant, not to be influenced by any of the connotations which the British listeners are aware of, with of course the exception of the Cockney and BBC accents.

The results of this part of the experiment showed that this was indeed the case. The North American respondents did agree with each other about the accents they recognized, placing the BBC accent first. We do not believe however, that this was because the BBC accent genuinely *is* the nicest. It was just that this accent is so well known that it is probably impossible to find English-speakers who do not know what its connotations are. Strikingly, however, they placed the Cockney accent not tenth in terms of pleasantness, as the British listeners did, but *second*! Clearly, the London accent does have connotations for North Americans, but these connotations are very *different* from what they are for the British. We can suppose that they associate London with vacations and think of it as an interesting and welcoming foreign capital.

For the rest, there was no agreement at all among the North Americans about which accents of British English are the nicest, and there certainly wasn't any agreement between them and the English listeners. This makes it plain that when English people agree about finding Birmingham and London accents ugly, this is not because they actually are ugly in any absolute sense. We have to assume that these accents are found to be relatively unpleasant beause negative connotations exist for the large industrial area of the West Midlands where Birmingham is situated and for the large London conurbation. American listeners, who do not recognize a Birmingham accent when they hear one, who know nothing about Birmingham, and who probably don't even know where it is, do not find the Birmingham accent unpleasant at all. And everything they know about London leads them to find London accents highly attractive.

SPELLING PRONUNCIATION

One way in which the pronunciation of English has changed is unique to this century. This is the first age in which most English speakers have been able to read and write. This amount of literacy has combined with linguistic insecurity (particularly, we suspect, in the case of people who might be described as lower-middle-class) and a fear of 'making mistakes' (encouraged by schoolteachers) to produce the phenomenon of the *spelling pronunciation*. As we have noted, English spelling is a rather bad indication of how English is pronounced and is a much better indicator of how English used to be pronounced in medieval times. Nevertheless, because of the prestige of the written language, the practice has grown up, as we have just seen, of using spelling to justify the 'correctness' of certain pronunciations, such as 'hammer' versus 'ammer'. Therefore, people who are worried about whether their pronunciation is 'correct' or not these days quite often turn to the spelling for guidance.

In the case of a number of words, this has led to complete, and sometimes drastic, changes in pronunciation. For instance, until the 1920s, everybody in England used to pronounce the word *forehead* as 'forrid'. Now the only people who do this are older aristocrats, who are secure enough in their social position not to worry about 'correctness', and older lower-class speakers, who don't care about what others think. Nearly everybody else says 'for-head'. Similarly, these days *often* is often pronounced 'off-ten' rather than the older 'offen'; *handkerchief* as 'hankerchief' rather than the older 'hankercha'; and *waistcoat* as 'waiscoat' rather than 'weskit'. Place-names are particularly prone to suffer from this form of linguistic neurosis. *Ipswich*, for example, always used to be pronounced 'Ipsidge', but, since at least the 1930s, nearly everyone has called it 'Ipp-switch'. And names like *Horsham* are now usually pronounced with a *sh* sound, although the earlier pronunciation was 'Hors'm' (the name comes from *horse ham* meaning 'homestead where horses are kept'; *ham* is the older form of the modern word *home*).

PATHOLOGICAL PRONUNCIATION

There is one type of pronunciation that we would agree is worthy of correction. This is the pronunciation of people who have some kind of language handicap and who can benefit from the work of speech therapists. These include deaf people, people whose speech has been impaired as a result of brain damage because of a stroke or accident, and younger children who are suffering from language delay. Sometimes problems affecting pronunciation can be major. Sometimes, particularly with younger children, they can be relatively minor, affecting perhaps only a single consonant, such as *th* or *r*, or one type of articulation. (There are many children who need help in pronouncing *ch* and *j* in English, for instance.)

One thing, however, is worth noting about speech defects. The answer to the question 'When is a speech defect not a speech defect?' is *When everybody has it!* For instance, it could be said that a child in Aberdeen who cannot pronounce *th* and who therefore says 'fing' rather than 'thing' has a speech defect, albeit a rather minor one. The same thing could *not* be said of a child in

Bad Accents?

London, where the pronunciation 'fing' is a perfectly normal part of the local accent.

One final word: speech therapy must never be confused with *elocution*. Speech therapy is a medical science that deals with patients who have pathological difficulties of some kind with their pronunciation or with other aspects of their language. Elocution lessons are usually indulged in by socially insecure groups in a society – often the second-highest-status group – who wish to improve their social and economic status by acquiring the outward trappings of higher-class status, including an accent of higher status than the one they (or their children) currently have. Elocution, of course, is a symptom of the disease of discrimination against low-status accents.

8

CHANGE OR DECAY?

H AVE A LOOK at the following text, and see if you can understand what it says.

Her com Swegen mid his flotan to Norðwic, and þa burh
ealle gehergode and forbærndon. Þa gerædde Ulfcytel wið þa
witan on Eastenglum þæt hit beter wære þat man wið þone
here friðes ceapode, ær hie to micelne hearm on þæm earde
gedydon, for þæm þe hie unwæres comon, and he first næfde
þæt he his fierde gegradian mihte. Da under þæm griðe þe
him betweonan beon sceolde, þa bestæl se here upp fram
scipum, and wendon heora fore to Þeodforda

The chances are that you had very considerable difficulty in understanding very much of it at all – in spite of the fact that it was
written in English. The reason for this is that the piece, which is
from the *Anglo-Saxon Chronicle*, was written more than 900 years
ago, and since that time the English language has obviously changed
very considerably. We now call the language that was spoken
in England before the Norman conquest Old English or Anglo-
Saxon. Here is a translation from Old English into Modern English.

Now Sven came with his fleet to Norwich, and totally ravaged
and burnt the town. Then Ulfcytel decided with the
councillors in East Anglia that it would be better to buy peace
from the army, before they did too much harm in the land,
because they had come unexpectedly, and he did not have
time to assemble his troops. Then under the truce which
should have been between them, the army stole in from the
ships, and made their way to Thetford.

Change or Decay?

English is not at all unusual in having changed to this extent. All languages change through time in the same sort of way. In fact language change is one of the most fascinating and puzzling things about human languages. In all the languages of the world, some words are lost and others acquired, while others change their meaning or gain additional meanings. The sound systems of languages change too, and so do their grammatical structures. 600 years ago, as we have already seen, all English speakers pronounced words like *out*, *mouth*, and *loud* as 'oot', 'mooth' and 'lood'. Now, most of them don't. 500 years ago very many English speakers said *cometh*, *hath* and *saith*, whereas today most people say *comes*, *has* and *says*. It is one of our jobs as linguists to try to explain why languages do change in this way. Unfortunately, we are not actually very good at it.

We can understand how social, technological and political changes influence a language. If you compare the Old English text with the modern English text above, you can see that some words, such as *gehergode* and *gerædde*, have been replaced by others, in these cases *ravaged* and *decided*. The replacements are actually words that were originally French, but which have subsequently become part of the English language. We can explain this quite simply by noting that in 1066 England was invaded by French-speaking Normans. Other sorts of changes, such as those in pronunciation and grammar, do not seem to be motivated so much by external forces. These are more difficult to explain, although quite a lot of progress has been made. And we are particularly bad at explaining why some changes happen at certain times and in certain places, and not others. We are working on it.

Linguistic changes are an inevitable and natural part of all human languages. However, they tend to arouse strong feelings among certain sections of the English-speaking population when the changes are obvious enough for them to notice. These Canutes*

---

*The Dano-English king Canute is widely, if erroneously, supposed to have thought he was so powerful that by commanding the tide he could stop it from coming in.

who try, nearly always unsuccessfully, to stem the tide of linguistic change, discuss changes as if they were self-evidently bad and a sign of decadence and decay. This is particularly true of changes involving words, because these seem to be much easier to notice than changes in grammar or pronunciation. Even so, most changes probably slip by unobserved. We shall therefore concentrate in this chapter on words, although what we are going to say is equally true of pronunciation and grammar.

LANGUAGE CHANGE IS AGGRAVATING

Let us look at an example of a change in English which is typical of many others. One type of change that is sometimes opposed is the sort of meaning change which has occurred to the word *aggravate*. Modern English dictionaries give two different meanings for this word. One is 'to make worse, more serious, more difficult', as in

He aggravated the problem

The other is 'to irritate, exasperate, annoy', as in

He always aggravates me.

The dictionaries recognize both these meanings. The Canutes do not. They say that only the first meaning is 'correct' and that the second meaning is 'incorrect'. How do they justify this claim? They do it by saying that *aggravate* is derived historically from the Latin word *aggravare* 'to make heavier' (and by extension 'more serious'), which is in turn related to the Latin word *gravis* (heavy). They claim that for this reason it cannot mean 'irritating', and that using *aggravate* to mean 'irritate' is confusing.

The Canutes, of course, are the ones who have got it wrong. The fact that *aggravate* has two rather different meanings is no more confusing than the fact that any other word has two meanings. There are plenty of words which have two or more meanings. Is it ever a problem that *table* can mean both something to eat your food off and a display of numbers on a printed page? Is it confusing that *ring* can refer to both something you wear on your finger and a sound made by a doorbell? Does it cause difficulties that *to go* can mean 'to depart', as in *I'm going now*; 'to travel', as in *I'm going to London*; or 'to work', as in *The clock won't go*?

We don't think so. In the case of *aggravate* it is especially unlikely that there will be any confusion. This is because in the first meaning ('make worse') the verb will normally precede an abstract word such as *problem* or *situation*, while in the second meaning ('irritate'), it will precede an animate noun such as *me* or *the cat*.

He is aggravating the dog

cannot mean 'he is making the dog more serious', and

He is aggravating the situation

cannot mean 'he is making the situation exasperated'.

The Latin origin of the word is an interesting historical fact. But it can be of no relevance for the modern English language. Language is a social phenomenon. Words therefore mean what people use them to mean, in spite of what they meant at some earlier stage in history. The 'irritating' meaning of *aggravate* is the most common meaning in everyday usage and the one that most speakers learn first as children. An individual cannot unilaterally decide that a word means something other than the meaning that every other speaker ascribes to it, even if he or she brings a language that has had no native speakers for over a thousand years into the argument. The authors of this book could decide, for example, that *nice* really means 'ignorant', because as linguists we know that it derives from the Latin word *nescius* (ignorant). But, if we were to say to our worst students 'Because of your laziness you are very nice', it is absolutely certain that we would be misunderstood, and it is probable that our sanity would be questioned. Indeed, using the original Latin meaning of words could lead us to ridiculous claims. We would have to argue that a sentence like

She was a nice person who was inclined to have as her concern the construction of the finest projects

really means

She was an ignorant mask who was leant to have as her mingling the piling-up of the last throw-downs.

We do not think this would be a good idea.

Aggravate, then, is a word which came into the English language in the sixteenth century with the meaning of 'to make more serious'. Since then it has added to the resources of the language by acquiring an additional meaning 'to exasperate'. Interestingly, even more recently it has given rise in Britain to another word, *aggro*, derived from the noun *aggravation* and defined by *Collins Dictionary of the English Language* as 'threatening behaviour'. We think that it is interesting, however, that these useful developments in the language are regarded as undesirable by purists. Why should this be?

We think that in very many cases pseudo-scientific arguments based on 'confusion', Latin origins, and so on, are really rationalization for sentiments that are actually social in origin. In this case, the social origins of the prejudice against the newer meaning of the word *aggravate* have to do with the fact that the older meaning is confined to more learned and/or formal styles of speech and writing. In contrast, the newer meaning is usually found only in more colloquial and casual styles. The newer meaning therefore tends to have lower prestige and to provoke less favourable reactions from those who are more inclined to devalue informal language.

<u>HOPEFULLY THERE WILL BE NO CHANGES</u>

Another word which has undergone an extension in meaning even more recently is *hopefully*. Until the 1970s, people in Britain who were interested in such things might have told you that this word was treated differently in British and American English. In British English, *hopefully* was only a manner adverb which described how somebody was doing something:

> *She sat there hopefully*

meaning 'She sat there in a hopeful manner'. It had this usage in American English too, but American English had an additional usage in which the word *hopefully* modified the whole sentence, as in

> *Hopefully it won't rain tomorrow*

which means 'It is to be hoped that it won't rain tomorrow'.

This is quite a normal state of affairs in the English language. We have a large number of adverbs which operate in this way. *Naturally*, for instance, is a manner adverb in

> *He acted naturally*

but a sentence adverb in

> *Naturally I'll do it.*

Similarly,

> *She sang sadly*
> *Sadly, I can't come*
>
> *They played happily*
> *Happily he came on time*

and so on. Since the language operates in this way, it was not at all surprising when the formerly American-only usage also began to appear in the speech of British people at the beginning of the 1970s. This was probably due partly to American influence and partly to natural linguistic change, with the already well-established adverbial pattern extending to include *hopefully* as well as *happily* and the like.

Now, when this new usage began to become widespread in Britain, around 1974, the Canutes began to get angry about it. They wrote letters to the BBC and to newspapers complaining about 'this barbaric Americanism', 'this corruption of the language' and so on. Interestingly, they also complained about potential confusion between the old *hopefully* and the new *hopefully*, although it is clear that there could be none, just as there is none with the two types of *naturally* or the two types of *sadly*. By 1980, it was clear that their battle had been lost. From 1974 until about 1978 it was possible to talk to first-year linguistic students at British universities about this linguistic change and the passions it had aroused since they had observed it and found it interesting. After that, however, this was no longer possible. By 1980, British nineteen-year-olds had no recollection whatsoever of a time when *Hopefully it won't rain* was not a possible construction. They expressed amazement that this could ever have been so. 'What did you say before?' they would ask.

This then was a very rapid change indeed, and one which affected the speech of millions of people. It is clearly here to stay. Why did some people find it so objectionable? Note that it was very difficult for them to find coherent and rational arguments against this usage, just as it had been for Americans a decade or two earlier who had objected to the usage in the United States. Obviously it is difficult to find good arguments against something which speakers find so desirable and/or useful that tens of millions of them adopt it very rapidly. In the end, many of the objectors were reduced to saying simply that they *did not like it*. Why not? The answer to this interesting question, we believe, is that the Canutes didn't like it *because it was new and different*. We are not psychologists, and we do not have any profound or elegant explanations for where feelings of this sort come from. But it is a matter of common observation that there will never be any innovation of any sort that someone somewhere will not object to. New and alien things, especially if they are associated with a different age group, can often seem threatening or objectionable until you get used to them.

GAINS AND LOSSES ON THE WORD MARKET

In both the cases we have just looked at, the words in question have acquired additional meanings. Other types of change also occur. For example, words can also lose meanings. This process is equally common, but it attracts much less attention from the purists, for the obvious reason that it is hard to notice. Does anyone, for instance, object to the fact that *haughty* no longer means 'noble, exalted'? We don't think so. And this is equally true of the total loss of old words as opposed to the introduction of totally new words into the language. Very few purists will lament the fact that English speakers no longer use words such as *dulcify*, but there are plenty who will deplore the introduction of new words such as *businesswise*.

A further type of change that can affect the meanings of words is the process of *weakening*, which typically affects words with a rather high emotional loading. It too is often deplored by purists. Words such as *fantastic, fabulous, incredible, brilliant, amazing* began by having rather strong and dramatic connotations, but as a result of frequent use have come in modern usage to mean something very tame such as 'very good'. Does this matter? We don't think so. The fact is that all languages have very large vocabulary resources. Adult native speakers of English know between 50,000 and 250,000 words, and it is not difficult for them to find replacements. And speakers of all the world's languages are very creative. As soon as a word loses too much emotional force to be effective, it will be replaced by another.

Even the language of modern purists will undoubtedly contain examples of words which have been weakened in this way over the centuries. Do they think that the language of modern teenagers is *awful*? Well, *awful* is an obvious example of a word which has been weakened in its meaning. Dictionaries define *awful* as 'nasty, ugly', but its original meaning, dating from around the thirteenth century, was 'inspiring awe, reverence or dread'. Does it make any difference to anything important that *awful* now means simply 'very bad' and not 'inspiring awe'? Hardly. The word itself has lost the original meaning, but the language continues to be able to express this meaning without any difficulty whatsoever. We can, for example, refer to something as *awe-inspiring* or *awesome* in order to express the same sentiments.

Languages are very resilient systems, and change in one part of the system will normally lead to a compensating change elsewhere in the system, if one is needed. Guardians of purity have no need to worry. Languages have always taken care of themselves in this way and will undoubtedly continue to do so. Very many words that all of us use today, and which do not arouse any controversy, are nevertheless the result of changes to their meaning which have occurred over the last several centuries. This is normal. We can cope with it, and the language can cope with it.

'When I use a word,' Humpty Dumpty said, in a rather scornful tone, 'it means just what I choose it to mean – neither more nor less.'

Lewis Carroll, *Through the Looking-Glass*

MRS MALAPROP – ONE OR MILLIONS?

However, this does not necessarily mean that small problems do not occur from time to time. Sometimes there is potential for confusion, but usually only minor. And sometimes disagreements can arise. There are two different types of change in meaning. The first is the sort of gradual change over the centuries which has been experienced by *awful*. The second type we can call a *malapropism*. Malapropisms are so called after the character Mrs Malaprop in Sheridan's play *The Rivals*. Her name was derived by Sheridan from the word *malapropos*, which means 'inappropriate'. Mrs Malaprop constantly confused and misused long, learned words. A malapropism is thus an unintentional misuse of a learned word through confusion with other, similar-sounding words, as in

The steam is causing condescension on the windows

If a single person such as Mrs Malaprop misuses a word, this is a problem for her. As we have seen, languages are socially based systems and individuals cannot unilaterally decide to change the meaning of words. In the case of Mrs Malaprop herself, the usual effect is comic, but of course confusion could also result. The moral is that trying to use fancy language can quite easily lead somebody into looking very foolish. Mrs Malaprop would have been much better advised to stick to her own everyday language.

Notice, however, that if everybody used the same malapropism, then it would by definition no longer be a malapropism. In the very highly unlikely event of all speakers of English coming round to using *condescension* in the meaning of 'condensation', no confusion would be possible, and Mrs Malaprop would no longer be comically in error. The fact is that words mean what speakers use them to mean. Formerly, for example, all speakers of English, as we noted above, used the word *nice* to mean 'ignorant, foolish'. Gradually the usage went through a series of changes so that the meaning became by turns 'shy', 'delicate', 'fine', and finally 'pleasant'. Anyone wanting these days to use *nice* with its original meaning would be making just as bad a mistake as Mrs Malaprop.

However, *while* words are changing their meanings, confusion may arise in some cases. This is true particularly if the change is a type of malapropism/misinterpretation rather than gradual change. Even in many of these cases, misunderstanding is actually unlikely. For instance, the English language has a word *interested* which has two different meanings, deriving from the fact that the word *interest* itself also has two meanings. The first *interested* uses the earliest meaning that the word had when it was introduced into English in the fifteenth century. The meaning is 'being personally involved', as in

I am an interested party in this dispute.

The second, later but now more common meaning, is approximately 'showing or feeling curiosity about something' – the opposite of *bored*, as in

I'm very interested in football.

The fact that the word has these two meanings is not felt by any English-speaker to constitute a problem, and confusion never seems to arise.

However, the negative form of *interested* in its first meaning is, according to the dictionaries, *disinterested*, which therefore means 'impartial, not having any personal involvement'. The negative form of *interested* in its second meaning, on the other hand, is *uninterested*, which therefore means something like 'bored, feeling no interest or curiosity'. There is thus a distinction in the negative which is not available in the positive:

You're an interested party but I am disinterested and therefore more objective about it

versus

Change or Decay?

You may be interested in this but I am utterly uninterested in gardening programmes.

However, the word *interested* in its original meaning, together with its negative counterpart *disinterested*, is a rather learned and formal word in English. Most speakers would probably use words such as *involved/not involved*, *biased/unbiased*, *neutral/not neutral* instead. This has led, particularly in more recent years, to a 'misuse' of the form *disinterested* by many English-speakers, who now use it to mean the same thing as *uninterested*.

I'm disinterested in gardening.

This is not a surprising development. There are a number of reasons why we should not be surprised. First, the prefix *dis-* is very frequently used in English to form negative adjectives out of positive ones, as in *disagreeable, disarmed, dishonest*. It is therefore not at all astonishing that speakers should begin to prefix it to the word *interested* also. Secondly, a number of advantages follow from this development. For instance, two words are now available for common usage in the language where originally there was only one. It is already fairly clear that this has been taken advantage of by the speakers who have this new usage (and they are almost certainly now in a majority). The fact is that *disinterested* is often now used to refer to a positive lack of interest, as opposed to the mere indifference indicated by *uninterested*. If you are *disinterested* in something, you are *really* uninterested in it. Another advantage is that we now have a noun to correspond to the adjective. The English language did not formerly have a word *uninterestedness* or *uninterest*, but now we can say, if we have accepted this innovation,

The pupils demonstrated considerable disinterest in their lesson

Previously, we would have had to use a phrase such as *lack of interest*. Thirdly, for most speakers of English there was no possibility of confusion arising out of this new usage since they never used *disinterested* in its original meaning anyway.

But what about those, perhaps more educated people who *did* use *distinterested* in the original way? Can there be any confusion for them? It does not seem so. Just as confusion does not arise over the two meanings of *interested*, so no confusion arises over the two meanings of *disinterested*. In most cases, context will normally make it clear which meaning is intended. We do not feel that

You look disinterested

is ambiguous, and we also feel that

You're a disinterested party

is perfectly clear.

As we saw above, the answer to the question 'When is a malapropism not a malapropism? is 'When everybody uses it.' If, in a hundred years' time, every English-speaker uses *disinterested* in this new way, as they probably will, we shall no longer be able to speak as we did above of 'misuse'. The word *disinterested* will no longer be unambiguous, of course, but for the most part no problems will arise, and the language will have gained in other ways instead. It is true that the change may have arisen in the first place out of ignorance, and even perhaps out of a snobbish desire to use a more high-faluting word than *uninterested*, but, although this may perturb some of our pedants, it will not perturb the language.

Even now it is not entirely clear that we are justified in talking of 'misuse'. Clearly, Mrs Malaprop, who was in a minority of one, misused words, as anyone can who has misunderstood how everybody else uses a word. Children are particularly prone to this, of course. Equally clearly, if a time comes when every single English-speaker uses *disinterested* in this new way, we would be completely unjustified in talking of 'misuse', just as today we would be totally unjustified in claiming that 300 million native English-speakers 'misuse' the word *nice* because it 'really' means 'foolish'. But what about the current situation concerning *disinterested*? If a majority of English-speakers use *disinterested* to mean *uninterested*, but the dictionaries and grammar books tell us, in the words of the *Collins English Dictionary*, that 'careful writers and speakers avoid this confusion', is this 'misuse'?

Actually, 'misuse' is probably too simple a term to apply to a complex and fluid situation like this. There is a scale or continuum ranging from *misuse* to *use*. When the first person adds a new meaning to an old term, this is misuse, conscious or unconscious. When everybody employs the new meaning, as with *nice*, this is use. But it is not meaningful to look for a particular point in time, or for a particular point on the scale, where misuse becomes use. What we can certainly say is that, at the moment and for the time being, there are certain social situations and certain sorts of writing where it is sensible, if one wishes to gain the approval of certain others, to avoid using *disinterested* in its newer sense.

CONFLICTING MEANINGS

In a small number of cases, however, difficulties can occur. If everybody agrees about the original meaning of a word, no problems arise. If, at some later stage, everybody agrees about a newer or additional meaning for a word, again no problems arise. But what about if intermediate stages occur when people don't all agree?

One recent example of this from English concerns the word *chauvinist*. Nicolas Chauvin was one of Napoleon's French soldiers who was notorious for voicing his mindless nationalism long and loud. His name thus gave rise to the term *chauvinism*, which meant 'fanatical, mindless nationalism'. A person who demonstrated such irrational belief in the superiority of his or her own nation could therefore be called a *chauvinist*. This is what this word meant until quite recently, although it was never in particularly common usage.

However, with the rise of the feminist movement came the

development of the new term *male chauvinist*. Obviously, a *male chauvinist* was a (male) person who irrationally believed in the superiority of male human beings over female human beings. Since this was a common phenomenon, this term became very useful indeed and was used very frequently, to the point where it became convenient to abbreviate it to *chauvinist*. For many speakers today, therefore, *chauvinist* has become a shorthand way of saying *male chauvinist*. However, there are also people who had never come across the older meaning of *chauvinist* as 'nationalist' and for whom therefore *chauvinist* can *only* mean *male chauvinist*. Confusion *can* therefore arise. If we meet someone who is a rabid and obnoxious nationalist and we want to refer to him as a *chauvinist*, we do run the risk of being misunderstood by some people who don't know the older meaning and who will think that we believe him to be a male supremacist.

A similar problem has recently affected the word *billion* in British English. Until recently, *billion* meant 'a million million' (1,000,000,000,000) in Britain, but only 'a thousand million' (1,000,000,000) in the United States. Since most of us never had very much cause to talk about a million anythings, this was not a serious problem. *Billions* simply meant an enormous number of something, and whether there were nine or twelve noughts on the end hardly mattered. Inflation has meant, however, that American financiers these days often find themselves talking about 'a billion dollars'. And now British financiers have followed suit. So, although you always know what Americans mean if they say a *billion*, you can never be sure now what British people mean if they say the same thing. If you hear someone talking of a *billion* in Britain, there is now always the chance that you will misunderstand them by 999,000 million. This might, we suppose, be inconvenient sometimes.

A FACT OF LIFE

Linguistic change is a fact of life. Very occasionally it can give rise to problems. Most often, however, it does not. Language change does not represent decay. Some changes may even represent progress, as when language changes occur together with social or technological changes. But mostly change is just change – an inherent part of language systems and as natural as change in any other sphere of human existence. It could be argued, of course, that language change is inevitable but unfortunate. For example, it is true that, were it not for the process of language change, we would be able to understand the writings of King Alfred without taking a course on Old English, and that we would be able to understand Chaucer without the help of school-teachers.

But notice that without linguistic change it would not just stop there. If there had been no language change for the last 2,000 years or so, modern English-speakers would be speaking the same language as those people who today speak German, Dutch, Frisian, Icelandic, Faroese, Norwegian, Danish and Swedish. (Sometimes the two authors of this book might have found that convenient.) And, if there had been no such thing as change in language at all, then English-speakers would today also all be speaking the same language as the people who speak French, Spanish, Italian, Russian, Polish, Czech, Lithuanian, Greek, Albanian, Persian, Hindi, Bengali, Panjabi and very many other languages. All these languages have descended from a common ancestor over the last several thousand years. (Whether all the languages of the world were once, long ago, originally all the same language, is a question we cannot answer. It can be proved that two languages are related but it can never be proved that two languages are not related.) The emergence of such a wide variety of languages is the result of many different linguistic changes in many different places. In fact, if it were not for the process of language change, we would not only all be speaking the same language, we would even all be speaking the same dialect. It is change in language that gives rise to differentiation between dialects in the short term and between languages in the long term.

LINGUISTIC AND CULTURAL DIVERSITY

Of course, in some ways it would be good to be able to speak to, say, Lithuanians without having to learn their language. But we are inclined to think that this would not be an entirely good thing, and that there are advantages to language change. Our own feeling is that language change is not only an interesting phenomenon, but has also played an important role in the history of the human race. Imagine a situation where the majority of people in the Americas, in Europe and in parts of Western and Southern Asia all spoke exactly the same dialect. For one thing, this would be very boring for linguists. But it would also be very boring in another more important way. We would like to argue that the barriers to communication posed by different languages are a good thing. They can be broken through, of course. People can learn to speak more than one language (most people in the world do), and communication between groups speaking different languages is perfectly possible. But the fact that there are these barriers to communication means that different groups of human beings can support and sustain different cultures, different values and different ideas, and survive as different communities.

This cultural diversity leads to different opportunities to develop alternative ways of exploring possibilities for social and technical progress. A world where everybody spoke the same language would soon be a world of enormously reduced possibilities and potential. Everybody would have the same kinds of knowledge, listen to the same range of music, wear the same sort of clothes, behave according to the same norms, and experience and interpret the world along the same general lines. This would not augur very well for the future of the human race.

In most parts of the world today the growth of linguistic diversity has slowed down or come to a halt. The tide is beginning to turn, with an increase in linguistic and cultural uniformity in many areas. The English and the Swedes today speak different languages because, many hundreds of years ago, their ancestors moved away from one another, were no longer in contact, and so their speech diverged.

Today, communications are enormously improved, and linguistic divergence on this scale is no longer likely to take place. We do not mean that Swedish-speakers and English-speakers will end up speaking the same language. Established differences between languages will remain, and, indeed, some increase in differentiation will continue. The English of Britain and America, for instance, will continue to diverge somewhat, although not to the point where communication is no longer possible. But, in many parts of the world, economic and cultural imperialism is beginning to lead to the extermination of many languages, especially those spoken by smaller, economically less powerful groups. If this process continues, the world will be a much more homogeneous place linguistically and therefore culturally. We regard this as unfortunate. All human languages are complex and unique products of the human mind. Once a language is exterminated, it can never be revived (unless, as with Hebrew, a tradition of knowledge of the language is somehow maintained in spite of the absence of native speakers).

We must also be thankful that language change has led to variety *within* languages. The English-speaking world would be a very different place without its range of accents and dialects. Dialect and accent are important badges of social and regional identity. If Americans, Australians, Yorkshiremen and Scots all spoke in exactly the same way, these badges would not be available. Language is a vital way of proclaiming that one is a member of a particular community and not of some other community. It acts as a glue to keep insiders together, and as a barrier to keep outsiders out. Dialect and accent give us an important feeling of *belonging*, and without language change we would have none of this diversity.

Language change, then, is in many respects a valuable phenomenon. Languages do not need to be protected from language change. All human languages are always changing, in pronunciation, grammar and vocabulary. This appears to be a universal characteristic of human behaviour. Modern English will probably not be very intelligible to English-speakers a thousand years from now, if there are any. There is nothing we can do about this (other than help to sustain educational systems where there is room for the study of ancient languages). Instead, we can look at the positive side and be glad that human beings are the flexible and creative organisms that they are. Changing language is not bad language. Change does cause a few minor problems, but most of these are problems only for those conservatives who do not like to see anything change. Language change is part of the human condition.

POSTSCRIPT: GOD OR DARWIN?

1 Does language change more today than it did fifty or 500 years ago?
2 Are the changes that occur mostly for the better or mostly for the worse?
3 Do children have better or worse language than children did fifty years ago?

We have posed these questions to a lot of people (mostly students and teachers), and a rather interesting pattern appears in their reactions. A majority seem to have ready-made answers to the questions. They believe that most changes are for the worse and that language is changing more these days than it used to. And they certainly believe that yesterday's children had better, 'richer' language than children of today.

The belief that the quality of language is deteriorating is not new. It dates back hundreds, even thousands, of years and is part of common linguistic folklore.

It is rather amusing to think about this from the perspective of the origins of language. There is no uncontroversial theory about the origin of language. At times it has been considered unscientific even to speculate about such an issue. There are a lot of ideas about language origin, but let us just outline two main theories in a rather general way.

One theory claims a divine origin for language: God gave language to the human race, and for thousands of years it has been our duty to use and protect this language. Most religions include a story of this sort.

> *In the beginning was the Word, and the Word was with God, and the Word was God*
>
> *John 1:1*

The other theory says that the development of language is an aspect of the biological development of the human species. This is a Darwinistic view on the matter. At the beginning, the language of humans was not so different from the communication systems of animals. Step by step, human language (and the human brain) developed into something more and more effective and efficient. With the help of language, human beings have conquered the world.

If we believe in the divine origin of language, it is natural to think that God gave us a true and perfect language. (We make no theological claims here and we do not want to say that Christian faith is incompatible with an evolutionary view.) In the hands of man, this language has changed and thereby degenerated. If this process of degeneration has been going on for thousands of years, we should be in trouble by now. One wonders when we shall reach the bottom and have to climb up into the trees again.

From a Darwinistic point of view, it is reasonable to believe that it is the other way around: we started from the bottom and have developed language into something better. It's getting better every day, as the Beatles once put it. These two views may be illustrated thus:

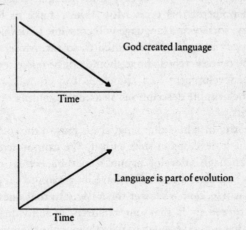

There are also some interesting combinations of these two ways of looking at things. There are people who in principle have an evolutionary view of the origins of language but who believe that the development changed direction at some point and started to turn downwards. When we have asked such people when this change occurred, we have found that the turning point is felt to be at the end of the nineteenth century, or in some cases in the period around 1950 and 1960. This would give us a graph like this:

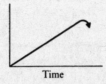

If this picture were true, we would truly be in the middle of an exciting period of transition. It sounds upsetting, but, if the fall is no quicker than the rise, we have a long way to go before we are back where we once started.

Actually, we do not believe that humanity has come to a transition point of this type. Most things make us believe that technology, society and language will continue to develop in much the same way as we have been used to so far. Moreover, graphs such as the ones sketched above should not be taken too seriously. Language development and change is too complicated to lend itself to such simple descriptions as arrows pointing upwards and downwards.

A fruitful insight is that language is part of the society we live in and that it develops in step with it. We cannot actually know whether language is developing into something better or something worse. As linguists, we certainly have no reason to suppose that it is getting worse, but, whatever the answer to that question is, we do have to see to it that our children as individuals develop language that is good enough to help them make their way through life. And most things in our modern technological society – the way it is becoming more complex, more literate and making greater educational demands – suggest that our children's language abilities have in fact to be *better* than ours.

9

BAD LANGUAGE AND EDUCATION

ONE OF THE things that we have been saying in this book is that we, as linguists, prefer to think of language not only objectively but also analytically. In educational situations, this analytical approach to different types of language, including those that are sometimes thought of as 'bad', can be very useful for teachers and pupils. It is very helpful, for instance, when dealing with varieties of language, to be able to distinguish between what linguists call *dialect, accent, register* and *style*.

SORTS OF DIALECT

Dialects are language varieties which differ from one another grammatically as well as in other ways. People who say *I ain't got none* are speakers of a different dialect from those who say *I haven't got any*. Dialects of English can be divided into two main groups.

Traditional dialects   These are conservative and often rural varieties that are more commonly spoken by older people. They are what people usually think of when they hear the term 'dialect'. Traditional dialects diverge quite considerably in their linguistic characteristics from Standard English and other mainstream varieties. Speakers in the west of England who say *Us byun't a-comin* (We're not coming), are traditional dialect-speakers.

Mainstream dialects   These are spoken by a majority of the English-speaking population and diverge much less from one another than the traditional dialects do. Standard English is one such mainstream dialect. The others, spoken by probably around

80 per cent of the population of England, are referred to as *non-standard dialects*. Speakers who say *We ain't coming* are speaking some nonstandard dialect of English; those who say *We're not coming* are speaking the Standard English dialect.

Dialects relate to both regional and social background. For historical reasons to do with, among other things, the location of the capital of England in London, nonstandard dialects spoken by lower-social-class groups and by speakers in the far north and far west of England differ more from Standard English linguistically than do dialects spoken by, say, lower-middle-class speakers from the south-east.

It is important to appreciate that all nonstandard dialects are just as grammatical as Standard English and have their own grammatical rules and structures. As we saw in chapter 6, for example, many dialects have a grammatical distinction not available in Standard English: the past tense form of auxiliary *do* differs from that of main verb *do* as in

> *You done it, did you?*

contrasting with Standard English

> *You did it, did you?*

In no dialect of English is it grammatical to say

> *You done it, done you?*

Well-known mainstream non-standard dialect structures found in very many parts of the English-speaking world include

> *I don't want none*
> *I ain't coming*
> *I ain't seen him*

> *She come home last night*
> *Them books over there*
> *We done it yesterday*
> *He sings nice*
> *A man what I know*

Teachers and speech therapists should also, of course, become familiar with regionally less widespread features that are found in their local area. This is essential to help them distinguish in children's language between dialect features, on the one hand, and actual mistakes and pathologies, on the other.

Lexical variation of course occurs within traditional dialects, with different words for scarecrow, for example (*mawkin, tattybogle, scarecrow, flaycrow,* etc.). But it is also found within mainstream varieties, including Standard English, for everyday things such as gym shoes (*plimsolls, sandshoes, pumps, daps,* etc.).

DIALECTS IN THE CLASSROOM

We think that teachers should encourage interest in the English language by teaching about traditional dialects, and by contrasting local nonstandard dialects with Standard English. Pupils, of course, will often be the experts on local speech. The grammar of both nonstandard dialects and Standard English should be discussed. The social and educational role of Standard English in modern society should be dealt with, and the benefits of mastery of Standard English stressed. It will be very important, though, for local traditional and nonstandard dialects to be seen as objects of interest and value rather than ridicule, and the usage of local speech forms should never be actively discouraged.

Pupils must be taught to write in the Standard English dialect for the social reasons that we have already discussed, especially for formal and public purposes. But of course there is no real reason why they should not continue to use their local dialect for, say, writing letters to friends, if they want to. Deviations from

Rural and urban speech

In Scotland today we find sharp contrasts in attitudes to rural and to urban speech. The reaction to rural Scots is often very positive: it is seen as 'good, old Scots speech'. Urban working-class speech, on the other hand, typical of the industrial areas in central Scotland, provokes general disapproval and is branded as 'slovenly' and 'degenerate'. This latter attitude became institutionalised quite early in the education system, so that we find, for example, at the turn of the last century comment from school inspectors about the desirability of excluding 'dialectal' and 'certain Scottish peculiarities' of speech from the schools . . . . Even the 1946 Advisory Council's Report on Primary Education in Scotland *contained the following reference to Scots . . .:* –

> *It remains the homely, natural and pithy everyday speech of country and small town folk in Aberdeenshire and adjacent counties; and to a lesser extent in other parts outside the great industrial areas. But it is not the language of educated people anywhere and could not be described as a suitable medium of education or culture. . . . Elsewhere, because of extraneous influences, it [Scots] has sadly degenerated and become a worthless jumble of slipshod, ungrammatical and vulgar forms, still further debased by the intrusion of the less desirable Americanisms from Hollywood.*

S. Romaine and E. Reid, 'Glottal sloppiness?'

written Standard English in formal work should be pointed out, not as 'bad English' or 'mistakes' as such, but as 'errors in Standard English'. The teaching of Standard English is also ideally best left until after other important writing skills have been mastered, such as punctuation, paragraphing, organization, logical structure and explicitness.

Everything we know from sociolinguistic research suggests that it would be *highly unrealistic* to try to make children who are not native speakers of Standard English *speak* this dialect in the classroom. Because of the social symbolism of language varieties, it is in fact no more likely that a majority of pupils will suddenly begin to speak Standard English than it is that they will acquire BBC accents. Teachers should instead concentrate on the active command of *written* Standard English. If they do that, they can rest secure in the knowledge that those pupils who wish, probably at a later stage, to convert this into an active command of spoken Standard English (by becoming bidialectal or by shifting dialects completely) will thereby acquire sufficient passive knowledge to enable them to do so of their own free will when and if they want to.

A speaker who is made ashamed of his own language habits suffers a basic injury as a human being: to make anyone, especially a child, feel so ashamed is as indefensible as to make him feel ashamed of the colour of his skin.
M. Halliday, A. McIntosh and P. Strevens, *The Linguistic Sciences and Language Teaching*

<u>ACCENT</u>

Accent simply refers to pronunciation, and all speakers by definition have an accent, as we have seen. Accent and dialect normally go together, but we distinguish them analytically because of the widespread practice of speaking Standard English with different regional accents. Teachers should be familiarized with the structure of different English accents because of the relevance to reading, spelling and speech pathology. They should also be familiar with the relationship between accent and social and regional background, and with work on attitudes and prejudices about accents.

Illustration and discussion of different regional and social accents, and attitudes towards them, are a useful and interesting part of language work in schools. There should be discussions of the importance of being comprehensible to speakers of other accents and to non-native speakers by, for example, reducing the tempo of speech and cutting down the number of fast-speech features such as elisions and assimilations. If you want someone to understand you, there is no need to try to speak with their accent – just slow down a little bit!

There is a very large degree of agreement among linguists that no attempt whatsoever should be made actively to change pupils' accents. Attempts of this sort normally fail, and succeed only in producing resentment and hostility towards language activities. This was recognized as early as 1878 by the Norwegian Ministry of Education, who made it *illegal* to attempt to change children's accents in the classroom.

We would suggest that a much fairer and more reasonable task for schools, in an era of wider mobility and greater ease of communications, would be to encourage pupils to acquire the ability to *understand* a wide range of English accents. Comprehension tests of this type would expose pupils to the full richness of the English language *and* improve their passive language skills. It is also of course much easier to learn to understand than to produce a new variety of language.

REGISTER

Register, as we saw in chapter 4, is a technical term from linguistics which simply refers to vocabulary and other linguistic characteristics associated with particular topics and activities. Different professional and other groups develop distinctive, often technical vocabularies. It is an interesting sociolinguistic question how far these technical vocabularies (often referred to as 'jargon' by outsiders) are actually necessary for the accurate discussion of a particular topic and how far they are simply a way of signalling in-group membership and keeping outsiders out. Do linguists need to use the term *lexeme*? Couldn't they just use *word* like everybody else? Why does a football *referee* correspond to a cricket *umpire*? It is certainly essential in geography to acquire the term *esker*, but is it essential in biology to acquire *clavicle* in addition to *collarbone*?

An extremely vital part of the educational process is the acquisition of the technical vocabularies for individual school subjects. It is therefore, of course, not just English teachers who should be concerned to expand pupil's vocabularies in this way.

STYLE

This technical term from the register of linguistics is concerned with language varieties as they can be ranged on a continuum of formality. Formality versus informality is most often signalled in English through vocabulary – compare *fatigued, tired, knackered*; *somewhat busy, rather busy, quite busy, pretty busy*. However, grammatical structures such as the use of the active versus passive voice can also be involved. *Slang*, as we have seen, is vocabulary that is highly informal and often associated with particular social and age groups.

Discussing the use of different styles of speaking and writing for different purposes and in different contexts should form a central part of English-teaching, particularly in secondary schools.

Pupils should also be exposed to a range of different styles through reading. A highly important task for the English-teacher is to increase pupils' repertoire of styles, in speaking and writing, through activities such as role play, and through a wide range of writing and speaking tasks, including some designed to raise sensitivity to different types of audience.

IMPLICATIONS

It is true that in Britain there is a tendency for more formal styles to occur together with Standard English, and for the technical registers of scientific topics (unlike, say, the technical registers of sports) also to occur together with Standard English. It is also true that high-prestige accents do not normally occur in Britain with nonstandard dialects. But there are no necessary connections here. It is important to appreciate the logical independence of dialect, accent, register and style. It *is* possible to speak Standard English with a Liverpool accent. It *is* possible to swear and use slang while speaking Standard English. *All* dialects are capable of being spoken in a whole range of formal and informal styles. There is *no* need to be a Standard English-speaker in order to acquire extensive technical vocabulary. And so on.

By way of illustration, we have drawn up a table of different versions of the same sentence, showing possible usages of standard and nonstandard dialects; high-prestige and low-prestige accents; technical and non-technical registers; and formal, neutral and informal styles. Note that there is no logical necessity to abandon low-status accents or nonstandard dialects in order to be able to acquire and employ learned vocabulary items such as *clavicle*. Note, too, that *E asn't bust is collar-bone* is Standard English, and that unstressed *his* is pronounced 'is' by all English-speakers in normal connected speech.

This analytical approach to the four main aspects of language variety can also be used in checking on pupils' progress in schools. It can help in distinguishing between usages which are 'bad' in

	STANDARD ENGLISH High-prestige accent	Low-prestige accent	NONSTANDARD DIALECT Low-prestige accent	
FORMAL STYLE	*He has not fractured is clavicle*	*E as not fractured is clavicle*	*E ain't fractured is clavicle*	TECHNICAL REGISTER
	He has not fractured is collar-bone	*E as not fractured is collar-bone*	*E ain't fractured is collarbone*	NON-TECHNICAL REGISTER
NEUTRAL STYE	*He hasn't broken is clavicle*	*E asn't broken is clavicle*	*E ain't broke is clavicle*	TECHNICAL REGISTER
	He hasn't broken is collar-bone	*E asn't broken is collar-bone*	*E ain't broke is collar-bone*	NON-TECHNICAL REGISTER
INFORMAL STYLE	*He hasn't bust is clavicle*	*E asn't bust is clavicle*	*E ain't bust is clavicle*	TECHNICAL REGISTER
	He hasn't bust is collar-bone	*E asn't bust is collar-bone*	*E ain't bust is collar-bone*	NON-TECHNICAL REGISTER

different ways and therefore require different approaches on the part of teachers. Suppose that the following (invented) example is a response by a child in an East Anglian school to an instruction to produce a piece of formal narrative writing.

> *When my father* come *home last night, he was really* knackered. *He sat in* are *lounge and watched* telly *all evening. I* done *my homework and then watched television too.* This operator doctor *was talking about the Health Service.* That *was* rarely *boring. Then there was the* one in charge of hospitals. *He* wasn't *very interesting* neither.

An analytical reaction to this piece of writing on the part of the teacher would differentiate between different types of error – different types of 'bad language' – along the following lines.

Bad Language and Education

1　The use of the *come* as the past tense is extremely common in nonstandard dialects of English around the world. In fact, this form is probably used by a majority of native speakers of English. In these dialects the verb *come* therefore falls into the same class of verbs as *put, cut,* etc.:

> *I cut some every day*
>
> *I cut some last night*
>
> *I come here every day*
>
> *I come here last night*

This form is nevertheless out of place in any piece of writing that is intended to be in Standard English. It is not bad grammar or incorrect English *as such*, but is clearly an error if Standard English is what is being aimed at. It is grammatically wrong from the point of view of Standard English, but it is grammatically correct from the point of view of the dialect.

2　The form *done* is the past tense of the full verb *do* in a majority of English dialects around the world. *Do* in these dialects therefore resembles the vast majority of English verbs in having no distinction between past tense and past participle forms, e.g. *I walked, I have walked*. It comes into the same class as irregular verbs such as *get* which do not have any such distinction either:

> *I got some last night*
>
> *I've got some every day this week*
>
> *I done it last night*
>
> *I've done it every day this week*

This usage in the East Anglian child's essay can be explained in terms of dialect interference. It is bad not in any absolute sense, but, again, only if Standard English was being aimed at.

Most East Anglian dialects employ *that* as the subject form of the third-person singular neuter pronoun, reserving *it* for the object position. Compare this with Standard English pronouns:

STANDARD ENGLISH	EAST ANGLIAN ENGLISH
he – him	*he – him*
she – her	*she – her*
it – it	*that – it*

So in East Anglian dialects we find a complete parallel between all the third-person pronouns, with different forms for all subject and object pronouns:

> *I don't like* him – he's *no good*
> *I don't like* her – she's *no good*
> *I don't like* it – that's *no good*
> *I don't like* them – they're *no good*

Also, *that's raining* is more usual in East Anglia than *it's raining*. This grammatical distinction appears in the East Anglian child's essay in the phrase *that was boring*, and thus is to be interpreted as dialect interference. Again, it is not bad – it is simply not Standard English.

He wasn't very interesting neither is not grammatical in Standard English, but is grammatical in nearly all other dialects of the language. Multiple negative forms of this type are therefore extremely common and to be regarded only as an error if the intention was to write in the Standard English dialect.

Bad Language and Education

ACCENT

1   In this essay the word *our* is spelt *are*. This, we agree, is bad spelling, although we are inclined to think that the English-speaking world emphasizes correct spelling rather too much and is too liable to ascribe all instances of wrong spelling to bottomless and invincible ignorance. This mistake, the teacher will understand, is quite natural because the local accent, like many accents in the south of England, has *are* and *our* with identical pronunciations.

2   Similarly, many East Anglian accents have no distinction between the vowel of *peer, dear, here* and the vowel of *pear, dare, hair*. This is why the word *really* in this text has been incorrectly spelt as *rarely*. We would like to stress that this is *not* a reason for trying to change this pupil's accent. If children anywhere in England have trouble in distinguishing correctly between the spelling of *meet* and that of *meat*, we do not automatically suppose that this is a reason to persuade them to acquire an old-fashioned Irish accent in which these two words are pronounced differently

There are lots of words which are pronounced the same and spelt differently – *pear, pair*; *see, sea*; *team, teem*; *sighed, side*; *led, lead*; and so on. We all have to cope with this. It is simply the case that which pairs of words cause this problem varies somewhat from accent to accent. In fact, the East Anglian child may have no difficulty at all in learning to spell *know* and *no* differently because in the local accent, unlike in BBC English, these two words are pronounced differently.

English spelling is actually something of a mess. We mean this in the sense that correspondences between pronunciation and spelling are rather complicated and sometimes quite irrational. We are not advocating spelling reform here, because to improve the orthography of English by bringing it up to date would be an immense and costly task, more so than changing over to the metric system, and on a par with changing from driving on the left to driving on the right. But it is worth pointing out that, once a reform that brought spelling closer into line with pronunciation was completed, this would make learning to read and write a much easier, less daunting and speedier task for English-speaking children, as well as for foreigners trying to learn the language.

Many languages do things much better. In Finnish, for example, where the spelling system is relatively new, if you see a word written down, you know how to pronounce it, and if you know how a word is pronounced, you also know how to spell it. Italian has no commonly used word *to spell*, for the same reason. Italian spelling is so rational that Italians simply talk about learning *to write*. Once they have learnt how to write, they have learnt how to spell – and that's that.

REGISTER

1 The usage of *operator doctor* in the essay suggests that the child is not familiar with the semi-technical medical term *surgeon*. The child's language is perhaps inadequate in that this particular word has not been acquired. But notice also the resourceful usage, typical of children, of language that they already know to express the intended meaning.

2 The use of *one in charge of hospitals* might indicate that the writer is not familiar with an appropriate technical term such as *Minister of Health*. Again the child can benefit from a widening of vocabulary. The language of the essay is not deficient in any serious way, and the child does already know and use tens of thousands of words. But here is a term that can usefully be added to the list.

STYLE

1 *Knackered* is a perfectly legitimate English word, but it is too informal for writing such as this and is therefore stylistically inappropriate. This does *not* mean that it is bad or inappropriate in *all* situations. Often *knackered* will be precisely the correct word to employ.

2   *Telly* is similarly a very common word in British (though not, for example, in American) English. But it is again stylistically wrong by virtue of being too informal. It is, however, 'bad' in this particular context, but not in all situations and at all times.

3   The use of *this* rather than *a* in *this operator doctor* is a common narrative device in informal story-telling, but is not usual in formal or even semi-formal writing. It is highly recommended for use in informal contexts, however.

4   The contracted form *wasn't* is utterly normal in speech and usual in informal writing, but consideration should be given to whether it has the right degree of formality in this particular case.

CONFLICT, GAP OR SLIP?

Another useful way of approaching the errors that children make in language is to distinguish between conflicts, gaps, and slips (Teleman 1979). A *conflict* occurs where children already know the rules of their language, but where this knowledge conflicts with the rules of some other variety, usually the standard. The cases we discussed under the heading of *dialect* come into this category.

For instance, children come into school already knowing how to form negative sentences in their dialect. It may, however, be that the standard variety does this differently. Teachers must remember in such cases that teaching English as a mother tongue is *not* like teaching geography or maths. We teach children geography and maths because they don't know them. We do not teach them English because they don't know it – if they didn't know English, we couldn't teach them anything at all! Here therefore, particular sensitivity is needed.

A *gap* on the other hand, occurs where children genuinely are ignorant of something and where this gap in their knowledge of the language can be filled. The items we discussed above under the heading of *register* are obvious examples of this. Here the teacher can add to children's knowledge in a much more straightforward way, by increasing their vocabulary.

A *slip* is where a child already knows something, but in the heat of the moment gets it wrong – a sort of slip of the pen. It is obviously important for teachers to be able to distinguish between slips and other forms of error because this bears crucially on whether children are perceived as actually knowing something or not. (Just because this is important, however, does not mean, as teachers will testify, that it is easy to do.)

Other forms of error that we do not discuss in this book, but which will obviously be of importance to teachers, concern errors of organization, logical construction, and punctuation. We hinted earlier that we do not believe that spelling is quite as vital as some people think. As linguists we would like to make it clear that we do believe that correct punctuation is very important indeed as a way of facilitating reading and understanding by indicating sentence structure. Knowledge of punctuation, of course, is not something children bring with them to school, and is therefore to be regarded as involving errors of the gap type.

VARIETY AS A RESOURCE

It is variety in language that leads to people making negative value judgements about other people's language. If everybody spoke in exactly the same way, there would be no complaints from anyone about 'bad language'. In an educational situation, however, this variety should be regarded not as a problem but as a resource. Most children are already very aware of language variety and language attitudes when they come to school, and they find it a fascinating topic for classroom discussion. Teachers who are prepared to take an open-minded, unprejudiced attitude towards the varieties of language spoken by their pupils will be the ones who also succeed best in fostering and developing children's linguistic interests and abilities. Adopting a somewhat analytical approach to various types of language difference, as discussed in this chapter,

Bad Language and Education

can help teachers to think not of 'bad' and 'good' language, but of language that is, in different ways, less or more suitable for certain purposes. This will help them and their pupils to develop a clearer idea of what is going on in the language and of how to develop children's language repertoires to their full potential.

Freedom from condemnation of nonstandard dialects, low-status accents and informal styles breeds an educational situation in which children can develop their language by concentrating on saying and writing what they want to say and write, without having to worry unduly and prematurely about how they are saying or writing it. We believe that children need to acquire the fullest range of language skills possible. Like adults, they need to be able to use language to be precise and vague, friendly and unfriendly, uninhibited and controlled, explicit and inexplicit, happy and angry, impolite and polite, refined and vulgar, amusing and serious, expressive and inexpressive, abstract and concrete, clear and obscure. None of these ways of using language is inherently good or bad in itself. Those human beings who can use their language to do and say whatever they want to do and say with it, regardless of what self-appointed pundits may think about *how* they do and say it, are the ones who speak and write language that is truly good.

10

MORAL

As we have seen, it is sometimes said that people today use bad or impoverished language. We also hear talk about 'verbal deprivation', 'poor English' and the like.

In our view it is totally useless to discuss language in these general terms. They are also dangerous because they are so vague. The only thing you can do is to ask people to be more precise about what they actually mean by such phrases. When they try to give examples, they normally come up with most of the things we have discussed in this book: slang, swearing, vogue words, bad pronunciation, nonstandard grammar, and so on. As we have tried to show, these things cannot be judged as bad of themselves and for all time.

> *For many years I have been disgusted with the bad grammar used by school-leavers and teachers too sometimes, but recently on the lunch-time news, when a secretary, who had just started work with a firm, was interviewed her first words were: 'I looked up and seen two men' etc. It's unbelievable to think, with so many young people out of work, that she could get such a job, but perhaps 'I seen' and 'I done' etc., is the usual grammar nowadays for office staff and business training colleges. ('Have Went' Saintfield, N. Ireland).*
>
> Quoted in J. and L. Milroy, *Authority in Language*

When young people are interviewed on radio or TV, they constantly run the risk of listeners' classifying them as having inadequate language. Is the older generation, comfortably relaxing in their living rooms, making a fair judgement? It is not easy to speak in front of a TV camera. Speech situations, in general, can be classified on a scale of informal–formal (or relaxed–uneasy). Being interviewed on TV is for most people as far as you can go towards the uneasy end of the scale. Naturally, nervousness will have an impact on our verbal performance.

Another equally important factor is our role in a speech situation. The strongest party in any uneven situation can often interpret the meaning of what is said in a way that suits him or her best. Take a typical school situation as an example. The teacher explains something to the class. Afterwards one of the pupils says, 'I don't understand.' How is this utterance interpreted? We can be fairly sure that the teacher and classmates take this to mean that the pupil is not clever enough or was not listening carefully enough to understand what the teacher said. The teacher has to explain it again, more simply.

Let us turn this situation around and have one of the pupils explaining a chemistry experiment. Afterwards the teacher says, 'I don't understand.' In this case the interpretation is completely different. A pupil who said or even thought 'All right, I will take you over it again so even you, my dear teacher, will be able to follow' would certainly be breaking the rules for this type of situation. A more normal interpretation would be that the pupil has expressed himself in a fuzzy and incoherent way and has to try again. In both cases, then, the blame falls on the pupil.

Many speech situations are uneven. The big and/or powerful person speaks with, at or to the small and/or weak person, who says something only when this is called for. This is a question not so much of physical size as of the hierarchy of roles involved. Here are some examples of uneven speech situations which should make the point clear.

THE STRONG PARTY	THE WEAK PARTY
teacher	pupil
doctor	patient
adult	child
journalist	interviewee

We do not claim that in one stroke we could make all speech roles equal. Some animals will always be more equal than others. Differences in knowledge about professional matters lead us to prefer the teacher's or doctor's word over the pupil's or patient's. But this advantage of greater knowledge in one area should not give a person permission to exercise power over others in all areas, or to talk over the heads of their listeners.

We certainly would like to see greater equality in communication between individuals, but we admit that the desire for equality can be taken too far. We heard of a young student in need of the toilet who asked his education professor, 'Excuse me, where can I find a toilet?' The answer he received was 'Well, what do you think yourself?'

It is not surprising that uneven speech situations have an effect on language use. Labov has given a striking example in *Language in the Inner City*. An adult white interviewer holds an object in front of a little black boy and instructs, 'Tell me everything you can about this.' 'A jet?' answers the boy, after a long silence, in a low voice and with clear question intonation. He is on the defensive. His intonation signals 'Are you satisfied with my answer?' No one can accuse him of having inadequate language – he is just being careful in a threatening situation.

When young people are interviewed on TV, then, they are in every respect the weak party. They are young, they are being interviewed, and they are perhaps being asked about something which they do not know very much about – for example, racism, unemployment or young people's fears about nuclear weapons. In such situations, it should not be surprising if they have problems expressing themselves. Besides, most people get nervous in front of a TV camera, no matter how professional they are. Ask us!

EVALUATING LANGUAGE ABILITY

The moral of this is clear. If you really want to know what people can do with their language, how competent they are as language-users, you should not base this judgement on an uneven situation where they obviously are the weaker parties. You do not test how good a football-player is by having him play in skiing boots. Someone might say that we ought to be able to learn to play in skiing boots, high-heeled shoes and all kinds of shoes – that is, we ought to learn how to handle even the most formal and nerve-racking speech situations. This is true. What we are suggesting is simply that we should base our evaluations of people's linguistic abilities on situations where they have a chance to show what they are really capable of. Even Bobby Charlton might miss a penalty kick in high-heeled shoes.

Another important point (maybe the most important of all) is that we should always spell out the criteria we are using in judging other people's language. We refuse to agree that there is any such thing as impoverished language as such. Sweeping generalizations can usually be attacked, and in this case we feel it is our duty to do so. Language cannot be impoverished in general. If it is impoverished, something particular in its use must be deviant or unsatisfactory in some way. And it really should be up to the accuser to explain what precisely it is that is lacking.

We do not want to claim that no one anywhere ever has language problems. There are lots of people who need to develop their skills in using language in speaking and in writing. However, it certainly doesn't help such people to tell them that their English is poor, especially since most claims of that sort are based on prejudice and misconceptions.

Also, judgements about a persons' language often are taken as judgements about that person in general. If someone says that your language is inadequate, that you have impoverished language, there is a clear risk that you may think they mean that you are lacking as a human being.

So, should we recommend that children's language ought not

Moral

to be tested at all, since a bad result might be taken as a general characterization of the child's abilities? We do not think one has to go that far. On the other hand, it is important to think carefully about what language tests test. Often tests points only to symptoms of language problems, and it is not always easy to figure out the causes behind the symptoms. Besides, test situations are always special and unnatural in some way or other, so we must draw conclusions from them with care.

LOOKING BACK

This book has been about bad language. It has not been our aim to list every aspect of language use which could possibly annoy a reader or listener. Such a list is probably impossible to make. Instead, we have tried to include a variety of examples of 'bad language', since we are mainly interested in discussing the principles that lie behind the condemnation of such language.

The book has therefore been about language ideologies, i.e. all those attitudes in large as well as in small things about language that we come across in our speech community. Everyone, every single person, has an ideology of language, although not everyone is aware of it. We have tried to talk about some of the more common ones in this book.

The main danger with bad language is that it may awaken our *acquired irritation*, i.e. the irritations we have learned to feel when we meet certain expressions in language (Teleman 1979). People have all kinds of strange ideas. Someone may reason that, if you cannot spell, you cannot talk or perhaps think straight; another, that if you cannot talk without swearing, you have nothing to say. We have tried to show that these generalizations are wrong. But they are common, so everyone has to be aware of this and use 'bad language' with care.

This book has tried to influence and change many widespread ideas about language. We have tried to show that the official, standard English language, in its British, American or any other form (even the Queen's English) is *not* sacred, but merely owes its status to a whole series of historical accidents. Historically, English has been influenced, in some cases rather strongly, by Latin, Scandinavian, French, Dutch and to a lesser extent many other languages. The English of today would have been quite different, if, for example, the Battle of Hastings in 1066 had been won by the English, if Nelson had been defeated at Trafalgar, or if the Second World War had ended in quite a different way. And what would have been the effects on English if Edinburgh had been the capital of Great Britain?

It has also been our aim to point to the value of natural and spontaneous spoken language. There is a tendency among linguists and people in general to use the written language as a yardstick against which to measure all types of language. This is clearly wrong. The spoken language is primary relative to the written language, in the development both of the individual and of the species.

If we can raise the status of everyday spoken language, we can hope for a better and more sober ideology of language. But there is always a risk of going too far in the other direction. If we can strengthen the status of local dialects, this will be a step towards greater linguistic democracy. But, if dialect fanatics were to take the place of the official-language fanatics who are in power today, we would only be building new walls to keep other people on the outside.

SUMMARY

Let us sum up the contents of this book using a number of maxims, with minor comments. These will be brief and sometimes slightly baldly stated. The arguments, discussion, and cautions will hopefully be found in the preceding chapters.

FLOWER GIRL OR LADY

LIZA. *I know. I am not blaming him. It is his way, isn't it?*
But it made such a difference to me that you didn't do it.
You see, really and truly, apart from the things anyone can
pick up (the dressing and the proper way of speaking, and
so on), the difference between a lady and a flower girl is
not how she behaves, but how she's treated. I shall always
be a flower girl to Professor Higgins, because he always
treats me as a flower girl, and always will: but I know I
can be a lady to you, because you always treat me as a
lady, and always will.

Bernard Shaw, Pygmalion

Keep science and opinions apart   This can be hard but it is
necessary. Every person has ideas and opinions about language
use. A certain construction can be viewed as good by one person
and bad by another. These opinions should be studied scientifically,
but they should not be made part of our theory of language.

'Badness' is not found in language itself but only in people's
views of the language   It is completely impossible to classify
constructions of language as good or bad on the basis of grammar
and language theory. It is only possible through a study of attitudes
to language. Bad language is what is judged subjectively to be bad
language.

Bad language is also language   Language constructions are
often classified as bad without any legitimate arguments. Many
things which have been discussed in this book, like *sort of* and
other small words, are perfectly natural ingredients in all types of
language use.

Moral

Bad language is worthy of study and discussion   Bad language cannot be stamped out by ignoring it. It must be dug out of the caves and studied. If we do this, we usually find quite normal principles of language behind the forms we investigate.

Language is constantly changing and so are our views of language   What was slang yesterday may well be common or even educated language today. Language use can never be frozen in a particular form. As long as a language is used, as long as it lives, it will keep on changing. Linguistic changes are not brought about at once. People did not wake up a couple of hundred years ago to find that the initial *k* was lost in the pronunciation of words like *knee*, *know* and *knight*. All changes start among groups of language-users and gradually spread from one group to another. For every change, there will be an intermediate period of variation in the speech community.

Where there is variation, there are attitudes to variation   There can be considerable variation in the use of language between different geographical groups, different social groups, different age groups and the two sexes. Everything which is judged to be 'bad language' will normally be found among those aspects of language which are involved in this variation. A word or a construction which is used by everyone will not usually be considered bad. No one gets mad about the definite article *the*, or the conjunction *and*. Not until these phenomena are used in an unusual way do we find them being classified as bad.

Both form and content get judged as bad   Words having to do with sex and defecation are good examples of things which are viewed as bad because of their content. Most things judged as bad in language, however, owe this to their form – slang, dialect, grammatical constructions and pronunciation.

Our views about language mirror our social and moral attitudes   Bad language has to do not only with our views about different aspects of language. It also mirrors our views about other people. Many things are considered bad because they are associated with people or groups of people we do not like. This means that much caution is needed when we are dealing with bad language, both as speakers and listeners. Different regional and social dialects can be seen as examples of this, as can slang and swearing. Maybe we should add another maxim: *You are not bad, mean or stupid just because you happen to use dialect, slang or swearing.*

It is not only what we say, but also how we say it, that matters   Most people probably think that the important thing is what we say, not how we say it. Unfortunately, reality is different. You will always be judged both by what you say and how you say it.

Language can be used to tell friends from enemies   Your use of language will reveal which group or groups you belong to. There are several shibboleths in language, in all languages. Each variety of language has its idiosyncrasies.

Bad language gives rise to emotions   You can swear and be criticized for it but you can also be applauded for it. Politicians can use swearing in official situations and, when they do, they certainly attract attention. They will be cited and they will appear on the news so they had better have something intelligent to say in connection with the swearing. The use of bad language can be efficient as well as dangerous. In our society, there is a general feeling that people should control themselves and their language. If an official person bursts out swearing, this may be taken as a sign of personal weakness. He therefore has to indicate that his words are planned and intentional.

Moral

Bad language can be amusing and friendly   'Bad language', in the form of slang, swearing and the like, can function as a pat on the shoulder. If the boss uses a more dialectal form of speech to a young employee, it is often taken as a friendly gesture. It can be one of many ways to show solidarity and strengthen a group.

Bad language can be offensive   'Bad language' can be aggressive. You can hurt people with it, and many people find it hard to defend themselves against verbal aggression. Of course, you can be rude and mean using any kind of language.

Style is relative   There is nothing like a given and definable sense or feeling of style. Style varies from century to century, from generation to generation, from one social setting to another. For those who want to be like others, it is essential to follow the style of all the other Smiths. It is not easy when the Smiths differ as they do.

It takes time and energy to follow the development of style. We see this best when we have been abroad for a couple of years. Then we realize how fast language changes. Should we worry about this? Do we all have to follow the fashions of language?

Fancy people have fancy slang   Well-educated people have their own slang – vogue words. These become very common for a short period of time, as they spread from trend-setters to trend-followers. These words are often based on established words, which in this process receive a new and more general meaning (*hopefully*, *hot*, *cool*, etc.). In this they are just like ordinary slang. The same people as condemn slang may indulge in extensive use of vogue words. It is hard to find any logic in this, but logic is not the strongest factor in our attitudes to language.

Vocabulary can be rich in many ways   It is often said the young people have small and poor vocabularies. We know for sure that their vocabularies are different from adults', but this doesn't mean that they are smaller or more restricted. Many new words are born among young people. Remember the synonyms for 'stupid'.

A word is not useless just because you do not understand it   We should not condemn linguistic expressions before investigating what they stand for and what functions they have. Young people have many expressions which adults do not understand. This does not make the expressions wrong, inappropriate or unnecessary. Dialects have many words unknown in the standard language. Linguistically, *troughings* is as good as its standard-language counterpart *guttering*. *Sort of*, *OK* and *well* are also words of the English language, even if they do not refer to concrete things, and they have specific, useful functions.

Language does not grow by banning parts of it   All human beings need a rich, varied and efficient language. We constantly have to expand the boundaries of our language abilities. Among other things, we do this by using new words and constructions. Our vocabulary is not enlarged by banning parts of it, like a handful of swear-words.

'Stuff and 'things' are no worse than 'phenomena' and 'entities'   We often think that some synonyms are more respectable than others. However, it is simply that synonyms can have quite different effects in different social settings.

We all think that our use of language should be placed at the right stylistic level, but no one knows what is right   Some things in language are taboo: for instance, religious and sexual cursing. But most things considered 'bad' in language follow the 'right level' rule. A little bit of slang may be charming, but there should not be too much of it. To use *sort of* a couple of times is only natural, but it should not become an obsession. And so on.

The problem is that what is the right level for one person is too much for another and too little for a third. Perfect linguistic behaviour becomes impossible – at least, if you want to please everyone all the time.

There is a lot of variation in all human languages, and we must accept the fact that not everyone uses language in exactly the

Moral

same way as we do. What right do we have to set up the language of our own little group as a criterion against which to measure all other varieties of language?

Your language is part of you The language we learn as children and grow up with will as a rule always stay closest to our hearts. It becomes an important part of us. Criticism of this language can easily be taken as criticism of the person as well as his or her social background. There are good reasons to be careful about criticizing other people's language, especially since we know that there are often hidden social and moral prejudices behind these judgements about language.

Children follow the models Many people get upset when they hear children swear. Actually nothing is more natural than children learning to speak the language spoken around them. Children do what we do, not what we tell them to do. And they have no problems in finding suitable models for bad language.

Your words mirror your life 'Tell me what words you use and I will tell you who you are.' It is not really that simple, but there is a lot of truth in this statement. As soon as we open our mouths, we reveal many things about ourselves, such as where and how we grew up, and which values we cherish.

We do not really know what our own language is like We often criticize others for doing what we do ourselves. Just make a tape-recording of your own casual speech. Listen to it, make a transcription of it, word by word, sound by sound, repetition by repetition. You will certainly find out a lot of things which you did not know about your own language. Don't worry – it's probably just as good or bad as everyone else's.

Bad language is no threat to civilization There is no reason to bring out the heavy artillery and claim that bad language (slang, swearing, dialect, etc.) threatens our society and civilization. 'Bad language' has always been part of our language and will be so in the future.

WHAT TO DO?

Society, culture and language change through time. Developments in society lead to changes in the language, but changes in language seldom change society. Orwell's Newspeak cannot be introduced before we have a society suitable for it.

Everyone should be given the chance to develop their language, but this is better done by presenting alternatives and possibilities than by giving restrictions and prohibitions.

One thing should be clear, however: *bad language is not only a question of language. It is a question of human beings, too.*

The moral of all this is that you should not just classify different uses of language as good or bad, right or wrong, without thinking it through. It is always a good idea to ask questions like the following:

Why do people use these expressions?
When are they used?
What function do these words have?
How do people react to these words and constructions?
Why do they react as they do?

This way of approaching 'bad language' is fairer to those whose language we are talking about and more interesting to those of us who are studying or thinking about the language. And, finally, it is far more fun to view language in this way.

BIBLIOGRAPHY

Aitchison, J., *Language Change – Progress or Decay*, Fontana, London, 1981.

Andersson, L. G., *Fult språk*, Carlssons Bokförlag, Stockholm, 1985.

Bernstein, B., *Class, Codes and Control*, vol. 1, Routledge and Kegan Paul, London, 1971.

Bühler, K., *Sprachteorie*, Verlag von Gustav Fischer, Jena, 1934.

Douglas, M., *Purity and danger. An analysis of the concepts of pollution and taboo*, Routledge and Kegan Paul, London, 1966.

Douglas, M. *Natural Symbols*, Penguin Books Ltd, Harmondsworth, 1973 (first published in 1970 by Barrie and Rockliff).

Edmondson, W., and J. House, *Let's Talk and Talk About It*, Urban and Schwarzenberg, München etc., 1981.

Gore, W., 'Notes on Slang', *Modern Language Notes* 11, pp. 193–8, 1896.

Haas, M., 'Interlingual word taboo', in D. Hymes (ed.), *Language in Culture and Society*, Harper and Row, New York, 1964.

Halliday, M., A. McIntosh and P. Strevens, *The Linguistic Sciences and Language Teaching*, Longman, London, 1964.

Howard, P., *The State of the Language*, Hamish Hamilton, London, 1984.

Jespersen, O., Progress in Language, Swan Sonnenschein, London, 1894.

Labov, W., 'The logic of nonstandard English', in J. Alatis (ed.), *Georgetown University Round Table on Languages and Linguistics 1969*, Georgetown University Press, Washington, DC, 1970.

Labov, W., *Language in the Inner City*, Pennsylvania University Press, Philadelphia, 1972.

Leach, E., 'Anthropological aspects of language: animal categories and verbal abuse', in E. Lenneberg (ed.) *New Directions in the Study of Language*, MIT Press, Cambridge, Mass., 1964.

Milroy, J. and L., *Authority in Language*, Routledge and Kegan Paul, London, 1985.

Bibliography

Montague, A., *The Anatomy of Swearing*, Macmillan, New York, 1967.

Partridge, E., *Slang Today and Yesterday*, Routledge and Kegan Paul, London, 1933.

Partridge, E., *Historical Slang*, Penguin, Harmondsworth, 1972.

Quirk, R., *The Use of English*, Longman, London, 1972.

Romaine, S., and E. Reid, 'Glottal sloppiness?', *Teaching English*, 9, 1976.

Rosenthal, R., and L. Jacobsen, *Pygmalion in the Classroom*, Holt, Rinehart and Winston, New York, 1968.

Saussure, F. de, *Course in General Linguistics*, McGraw-Hill, New York, 1966.

Schourup, L., 'Common Discourse Particles in English Conversation', Working Paper in Linguistics, No. 28, Ohio State University.

Spears, R., *Slang and Euphemism*. New American Library, New York, 1982.

Stubbs, M., *Language, Schools and Classrooms*, 2nd ed, Methuen, London, 1983.

Teleman, V., Språkrätt, Liber läromedel, Lund, 1979.

Trudgill, P. (ed.), *On Dialect*, Basil Blackwell, Oxford, 1983.

INDEX

Index

Index

Index